D0502679

Bigger tha

Bigger

American Lives Series | *Editor:* Tobias Wolff

than Life

A Murder, a Memoir

Dinah Lenney

University of Nebraska Press

⊗

A portion of chapter 5 originally appeared under
the title "Deal" in *AGNI Online,* agni.bu.edu.

Library of Congress Cataloging-in-Publication Data
Lenney, Dinah.
  Bigger than life : a murder, a memoir /
  Dinah Lenney.
  p. cm. — (American lives)
  ISBN-13: 978-0-8032-2976-1 (cloth : alk. paper)
  ISBN-10: 0-8032-2976-3 (cloth : alk. paper)   3602 - 0898 4/07
  1. Gross, Nelson, 1932–1997. 2. Lenney, Dinah.
  3. Murder—New Jersey—Case studies.
  4. Millionaires—Crimes against—New
  Jersey—Case studies. 5. Children of murder
  victims—United States—Biography. 6. Fathers
  and daughters—United States—Biography.
  7. Murder victims' families—United States—
  Biography. I. Title.
HV6533.N3A3 2007
364.152'3092—dc22   2006020054

Set in Monotype Dante by Kim Essman.
Designed by A. Shahan.

For Eliza and Jake

Contents

| Acknowledgments

Thanks to Benjamin Weissman, who got the ball rolling and to Kitty Swink and Diana Wagman who read and listened so well from the start. I'm grateful, also, to Amy Gerstler, Sue and Larry Rodgers, Maia Danziger, Kit Rachlis, Bill Ayers, Alanna Hamill, and Walter Owen, good readers every one. Susan Cheever, Pam Galvin, Stephen Molton, Bonnie Solow, Deborah George, Leslie Ayvazian, and Courtney Pledger believed in the book and passed it around. U.S. Attorney Stuart Rabner was an invaluable resource, as was my mother, Leah Lenney, a stickler for accuracy of detail and syntax, and I'm bound to acknowledge my uncles, Paul and Michael Gross, who made time to share their recollections. I can't leave out Janice Shapiro, Emilie Beck, Jack Arky, or Jim Krusoe, all of whom offered insightful critique, or Mary Lou Belli, for her unrelenting faith in the project and in me. Most recently I'm indebted to Sariah Dorbin, Erika Schickel, and David Ulin for their concentrated attention, and to Timothy Schaffert for his discerning eye. If not for the Bennington Writing Seminars, I don't suppose I'd ever have finished a draft. That said, Phillip Lopate and Sven Birkerts deserve a page of kudos all to themselves, as does the team at the University of Nebraska Press, most especially my editor, Ladette Randolph. And always, for patience and clarity, thanks and love to Fred.

r than Life

1 | Prologue

Eliza Wants to Know

Eliza wants to know about all kinds of sex.

"So what's your take on oral, Mom?" she asks. "Giving and receiving," she adds, climbing onto a stool at the kitchen counter.

Eliza is thirteen now. She's taking Health as a science in her seventh grade year, in a program for 210 allegedly gifted children at a local public school.

"Do old people have sex?" she wants to know. "No, no, Mom, not like you and Dad, I mean *old* people," she clarifies.

She wonders when, if ever, she will have a boyfriend and when, if ever, I think it will be appropriate for her to have sex.

"Don't worry," she comforts me, having confided that a girl in her PE class *might* be pregnant, "I know I'm not ready *yet*. But just tell me, Mom, when did you first *kiss* a boy anyway?"

Eliza wants to know, wants to know, wants to know.

Eliza reads the headlines in the *New York Times* most mornings with her orange juice and cinnamon toast. She reminds me over and over that she is more capable than I give her credit for—more mature, more deserving—and she daydreams about her own cell phone and her own car and colleges in cities clear across the continent.

"Did you ever smoke cigarettes, Mom?" she asks. "Did you ever smoke pot? Do you believe in marijuana for medicinal purposes? How do you feel about the death penalty? How do you feel about the Israeli settlements? We're democrats, right?"

Eliza scoffs when I warn or explain, suggest or advise. "I know, I know," she interrupts, and "I'm not dumb, Mom," she insists, and "You're overprotective," she says on a sigh.

I remind her every so often we live in a big, dangerous city and it continues to be my job to take care of her to the best of my ability, at least for the time being. Eliza knows the world isn't safe. She knows about war and famine and poverty and crime. She knows that thousands of children lost parents when the World Trade Towers collapsed; but she doesn't know, she doesn't *yet* know, that her own grandfather was murdered nearly six years ago, and I am not ready to tell her.

Jake, on the other hand—who is ten—needs not to know. He'd prefer us to stay upstairs until he falls asleep at night, rather than going down to bed ourselves.

"What worries you, sweetie?" I ask when I kiss him good night in the dark.

"Oh, you know, Mom," he says, "the usual. Kidnapping and robbery."

As much as Eliza needs the truth under most circumstances, that's how badly Jake needs to believe he is safe. He dreams about terrorists, about dark caves and abducted children. We assure him again and again that there are more good people than bad and that nothing will happen to anyone he loves.

Whether his fears are age appropriate I cannot say for sure. But I remember when I was a kid, asking my mother to promise me she would not die. "I promise," she said, and I wonder now, was she as uncomfortable making that sort of promise as she should have been? As I should be when I promise my son the very same thing? Because it's disconcertingly easy for me to shake off the doubt, the discomfort. For one thing, this is what my boy needs to hear, and for another, I believe what I say. How naïve, how arrogant, how foolish to tempt fate, to pretend even for a moment I can predict with any kind of certainty I will live to be old. But even knowing that the Towers came down, that we anticipate the *Big One* in Southern California every day, that breast cancer claims friends and neighbors with terrifying regularity, that there's a fatality on the freeway during every rush hour, that my own father was kidnapped and killed with a pocketknife—even so and in spite of all that—I intend to live practically forever, and any other conclusion is unimaginable, unacceptable as far as I'm concerned.

What is this utter denial of the facts, of the news, of my own mortality? Is this optimism? Is it part of my essentially American sense of entitlement? Should I be reading up on Buddhism and other eastern methodologies? In any case, it seems to go hand in hand with my unwillingness to accept that life could turn out to be anything less than wonderful—my indignation in the face of disappointment—my swallowing of turbulence and tragedy, and my faith in impossibly complete recovery after the fact. Nobody tells us when we're children that life is difficult and unfair. Instead we middle-class American kids were told that we could be anything we wanted to be, do anything we wanted to do. And we tell our own children the same. And sad as we are, scarred and uncertain as we are, we believe what we tell them. As a generation, as a culture, we're certifiable. We ought to be locked away.

"Mom," says Eliza, peeling the pink from under her nose, pressing it into the lump of Bazooka and sticking the whole disgusting wad back in the side of her mouth, "remember when Pop took us to the penny candy store and bought Jake the grape bubblegum you said he couldn't have?"

"Remember Pop took us on the golf cart and he let us drive?"

"Remember how Pop spun us so fast on the tire swing? Remember when he let us swim in our clothes?"

"I can't remember," Jake complains. "Even when I look at his picture, Mom, I can't remember Pop."

"Do him, Mom," Eliza prods. "Do him for us."

They say the voice is the first thing you lose—the first thing you forget—but I can hear him in my head, no problem, I remember his inflection, even better the tone, perhaps because it isn't so far from my own? It's true, I do my father well. The timbre of my voice is higher, of course, but I weigh it down, I find his cadence, I say:

"C'mon, let's pitch pennies, hey, hey, that's not the way you do it! You can't cry, you have to be a good sport, yeah, there you go, that's the way, you're a winner! A winner!"

They collapse with laughter, and Jake spills his juice.

For the longest time after my father's death, Eliza would blanch when I brought him up. "Don't talk about Pop, Mom," she'd plead. "Mom, please don't talk about Pop, I don't want you to cry."

I was determined, though. We had to talk about him, I reasoned, and crying was a good thing. I explained that if we didn't talk about him, we'd start to forget. And if talking about him made us sad, well then, that was perfectly okay. Crying isn't bad. Missing somebody isn't bad. Trying to catalogue everything you remember about someone you love isn't bad. And, of course, with time, I mentioned him less frequently, and after a while, when I did talk about him, I didn't choke up in the old way. Eventually I could say something like, "Pop would have loved to see you play basketball," or "Gosh, you look like Pop today," or "Pop would have laughed, Pop would have thought, Pop would have said . . ." and nobody would so much as blink.

It's not so much that I must tell my children what happened to my father, as that I must not keep them in the dark for too long. I must not *not* tell them. So how to explain to the loves of my life the truth of what happened to their grandfather? When do I say it? How do I insist that we hold up our heads and expect the best of people in spite of this terrible thing? How do I make them understand why I waited so long? How do I know when I have waited long enough? What to expect from Eliza and Jake, who cannot possibly remember very much about the man? Will they cry? Will they be fascinated? Repulsed? Or is it possible they will be largely unaffected?

I imagine it this way: I will sit them down at the kitchen table one morning. One weekend morning. Better to have this sort of discussion in bright light with a whole day stretched out before us, when we don't have to rush out to school or work at the crack of dawn.

I will come upstairs shortly after breakfast holding the large brown file with the torn clasp where I have stashed all the newspaper articles and condolence letters and court transcripts from September, 1997, through October, 1998, when the killers were sentenced. I will have organized the lot by then, put the papers in some sort of order—chronological, emotional—that will make sense to first-time readers. And I will ask my children to sit for a while with me, with us, before we all get on with our Saturday activities. Fred, my husband, is adamant that we tell them together when the time is right. Yes, the murdered man was *my* father. But they are *our* children, and he wants to be present and involved in this potentially traumatic exchange.

"I want to talk to you about Pop," I will say.

And when I say it this time, in this formal way in this formal setting with a fat, overstuffed portfolio on the table in front of me, the children will be intrigued, expectant; they will know something big is up. My stomach will churn, my heart will beat faster, maybe I will start to perspire and my hair will curl up behind my ears and at the back of my neck. I will hold tight to my package, pressing it closed at the top, wanting to reveal my evidence in my own time at my own discretion, wanting to choose which pieces, which articles, which letters to give them, which to read aloud and what and where to edit.

I will tell them the basics first. Gently, in a neutral, modulated tone. I will try not to be dramatic.

"You remember when Pop died," I will say. "You were too young to understand, but you're old enough now, mature enough, to hear what really happened.

"Pop went to work one day," I will begin.

2 | The Contents of the File

Letters of condolence.

Assorted obituaries.

My eulogy from the memorial service, handwritten on lined yellow paper.

Photographs taken from the top of the dresser inside my father's closet.

Eleven letters from my father.

Nine postcards from my father.

Transcripts of court proceedings.

Newspaper clippings, yellow with age, and copies of clippings, faded, barely legible on glossy fax paper, slippery to the touch:

"Millionaire developer is missing." The *Bergen Record*.

"Into Thin Air." The *New York Post*.

"Ex-Republican Fund-Raiser Is Reportedly Missing." The *New York Times*.

"New Jersey mogul disappears after withdrawing 20G." The *Star Ledger*.

"The way Gross vanished leaves FBI at a loss." The *Star Ledger*.

"FBI says kidnapping possible in vanishing of N.J. millionaire." The *Record*.

"Missing tycoon's car found." The *New York Post*.

"BMW's a dead-end in search for tycoon." The *Star Ledger*.

"3 Youths Accused of Killing New Jersey Restaurateur." The *New York Times*.

"Businessman's Killing Is Called Afterthought." The *New York Times*.

"Gross fired slaying suspect, source says." The *Record*.

"Gross' last day: memories and regrets." The *Record*.

3 | The Last Visit

May, 1997.

"Don't pick me up, I'm renting a car," said my father and sure enough he pulled into my driveway at dusk, wearing his favorite hat—straw, wide-brimmed, worse for wear—a rumpled blazer, khakis wrinkled from his afternoon flight, and a pink polo shirt with a coffee stain just under the strip of buttons. He put his clubs down across the coffee table and picked up the telephone to call his morning golf date, awkwardly hugging both grandchildren with one arm until he settled the phone between his ear and his shoulder.

I take credit for the mint on his pillow, but it was a friend's idea. I complained to her that he'd apparently come to play golf and not to see the kids at all. Join us for T-ball Saturday morning? Barbecue with us Sunday afternoon? No, no, impossible, golfing here, golfing there.

"How is it," I asked as I poured his coffee the second morning, "how can it be that you didn't bring gifts for my children?" I was so angry I couldn't look at him.

He gazed at me over the top of the newspaper.

"Oh," he said, going back to the headlines.

"Do me a favor," I said, "get them something, pick up something in the pro shop, okay?"

That night he came home with a plastic bag full of refrigerator magnets—painted porcelain fruits and vegetables, grapes, peppers, corn, tomatoes, cauliflower, cabbages—and the children fought for them like candy.

"You couldn't find a T-shirt? A key ring with a golf ball on the chain?"

The kids whooped over the magnets as though they were real toys, while I stewed in resentment. How dare he bring them refrigerator magnets? How dare they be so delighted just because that's what he brought?

"Did you find the mint on your pillow?" I asked the next morning.

He nodded and gulped his coffee.

"Very funny," he told the sports section, and he ate the oatmeal I made for him—with low-fat milk and raisins—in three large spoonfuls. The spoon shook a little in his trembling fingers (his Achilles' heel, you should have seen his signature on a check), then he pushed the bowl aside.

I still have the magnets. Some have fallen and broken in half, and a few must be buried in dust bunnies behind the fridge, but I have most of them, holding up carpool schedules, receipts, invitations, finger paintings and old photographs on three sides of my enormous side-by-side refrigerator/freezer. I'm glad now that he didn't come home with plastic golf balls or miniature clubs.

On the morning of the last day of the last visit, he and I walked down Princeton Avenue, our street, and took the stairs at the end of Baxter up to the top of Kite Hill. Just over the rise we entered Elysian Park, half walking, half jogging the four-mile loop.

The mustard was in full bloom, cascading fountains of tiny

yellow blossoms spraying out at us from both sides of the path.

"For God's sake," he shouted over his shoulder, passing ahead of me on the trail, "get off your toes, land on your heels, Jesus, you'll get shin splints, don't you know how to run?"

Back at the house, he packed his bag and his clubs, leaving three miniature bottles of Smirnoff behind, lined up between the Legos and Junior Monopoly in my son's armoire. ("We do have vodka," I told him, when he first unpacked. "We have very good vodka in the freezer, you know.") He donned the big straw hat with the hole in the brim—the one he bought for fifty bucks from my daughter's swimming teacher, just because he could, just to see the kid's jaw drop—and he let me walk him to the front door.

On the stoop outside, he kissed my cheek and did a double take.

"Why are you crying?"

I didn't say, *Because I couldn't look you in the eye for four days, I was so angry with you. Because you're trying to be nice to me. Because I don't know why your hands shake.*

"You'll never come back," I told him instead. "I don't know when I'll see you again."

"No," he agreed, "too much work to come here, too far from the course, Christ, it's exhausting."

He grinned. He loaded his clubs into the trunk, pulled out of the driveway and waved without looking, cruising down the hill on his way back to the airport.

4 | Missing

September 17, 1997.

In my daily calendar I crossed out an appointment with someone named "Helene" on the twenty-second floor of a building on Wilshire Boulevard. A temp job? A talent agency? I can't remember. According to my scribble I worked as a copy editor for a magazine called *Live* from 9:30 to 2:00. My father disappeared around 11:00 that morning, 8:00 Los Angeles time, while I was most likely navigating the traffic on the way to drop Eliza at school, a progressive public elementary clear on the other side of town. I must have left the magazine to pick her up that afternoon, without having to rush to retrieve Jake, since he apparently stayed after preschool for roller hockey, from 3:30 to 4:15. At 5:30 there was an open house at the Hollywood Los Feliz Jewish Community Center, where Jake was in his second year, having graduated from the Red Squares to the Yellow Triangles. Did we go? I can't remember. By 5:30 my father had been dead for several hours. All shudders, all extra-sensory spasms went unnoted; as far as I can remember I was hopelessly out of synch with what was happening to him that day in the northeast.

September 18, 1997. Back-to-school night, 7:00 p.m., says the datebook. Karate/Jake 2:30 to 3:30, also in black ink. Did Fred inexplicably take the kids to the school by himself? Why was I home alone that balmy evening, still light enough to be outside well after dinner?

Anyway, there I am, down three flights from the house, with the plastic yellow nozzle on the hose turned to full action, spraying fungus off the cactus that borders the neighboring yard and a corner of our plastic Doughboy-in-a-deck. I am wondering, I swear, if my father has returned from a golfing vacation in Scotland and thinking I will call him tomorrow or the next day; but this is no presentiment I'm feeling, no evidence of a spiritual connection, since he has been dead now for more than a day. Unless there is a soul, a spirit that hovers, reluctant to depart—unless he has wafted three thousand miles all the way from New York to whisper in my ear.

In any case I am deeply satisfied with my task—removing white blobs that stain my fingers burgundy if I touch them—finding healthy green paddles beneath the gooey rash. Ah ha! I am thinking of him because it was my grandfather, *his* father, who told me how to tackle the scourge the last time he was in Los Angeles, before he got too feeble to travel. My thoughts have wandered from the cactus to Grandpa to my father.

I'm grateful for this quiet time, for my ordinary life; only vaguely annoyed to hear the phone ringing up in the house, once, twice, four times before the machine picks up. I take my time, watering the roses and the hibiscus, washing the bird shit off the blue market umbrella, finally heading up the stairs to hear the message.

"It's about Dad," says the answering machine. This is my Uncle Michael's recorded voice, my father's brother, the youngest of three, and I'm confused for a moment. Whose dad, I'm thinking. My dad? Your dad?

"We're together in Hillsdale, call as soon as you can," and the phone clicks off.

Together means Michael, his wife Meryl, the middle brother Paul, and his wife, Gayle. My grandmother is dead, my grandfather, frail and suffering from dementia, lives in West Palm Beach, and my cousins are grown and live in their own houses with their own families.

"Your father's disappeared," says Michael when he picks up the phone, and he passes me off to Paul who explains that he's been missing since the day before and tells me, please, on hearing the panic in my voice, not to get hysterical.

My father had returned from his vacation in the British Isles and gone to work early that Tuesday morning. Tuesdays were his days at the office, the only time I could count on reaching him there now that he was semi-retired and had bequeathed the restaurant to his only son, my half brother, Neil. The restaurant, Binghamton's Ferry, is a huge boat docked on the Jersey side of the Hudson sharing an enormous parking lot with a bank, a couple of gift shops, and a movie theater complex, all rented from my father, the real estate baron. The office, last time I saw it, was a brown bungalow on one side of the lot, modest, and more than a little bit ugly. The floors slanted to one side and the ceiling leaked here and there between the fluorescent lights and the particle board. The summer I worked there, way back before my last year of college, there was a steady yellow drip from the air conditioning unit in the window behind my desk.

On that particular Tuesday, my father had been supposed to meet Noel, his wife, at a hardware store in Manhattan at 11:00. He'd never shown up. Earlier that morning, he was taped on the surveillance camera in the bank across from the ferry, where he took twenty thousand dollars out of his account. The teller recalled him asking his companion, a small, dark man in a hat, "How do you want it?"

My half brother, Neil, in the car on his way to work, saw my father coming the other way with two strangers in his silver sedan. Neil called the car phone, which rang nine, ten times until my father picked it up and said, "It's business, just business." The police were investigating, the FBI was involved, and someone had thought it time to call me.

It doesn't occur to me on the phone to be indignant at my status as an afterthought; I only figure out how galled I am after I hang up, when I realize more than twenty-four hours passed before they'd decided to clue me in. On the telephone, I rise to the news in a terrible rush, then collapse, as though carried and struck full force by the breaking of some gigantic swell. I fall apart. In this way I manage to insinuate my position as my father's first born; in this way, I want to believe after the fact, I've reproached them for their negligence.

"What should I do? What can I do?" I sob.

Paul says there is nothing anyone can do. I should sit tight; he will keep me informed.

5 | Just Business

In July of 1997, the summer before he was killed, I called my father to ask him for five thousand dollars.

"For what?" he wanted to know.

"For the house. To build a fence, to clean up the back, to fix the windows, stuff like that."

To live on, because we're suddenly, horribly broke, I didn't say, but I suppose he must have known all along.

"What's going on out there? Don't you people have any savings?"

"No," I shouted into the receiver. "We've had a bad year! Dad, please, I'm asking for help, Fred doesn't know I'm calling, he'd be mad if he did!"

"What the hell is going on out there?"

"Dad, stop it! I'm asking you to help me!"

"Dinah," he said, lowering his voice, "don't ask me to support you in a lifestyle you can't afford."

Six weeks later I learned he'd been ill. I'd never let a week go by before without speaking to him and now, of course, six weeks of silence, wouldn't you know, he was sick. I left messages for two days until I caught him at home.

"It's nothing," he said. "I'm 90 percent. I had Lyme Disease is all, took some antibiotics, and I'm better."

I told him, in a rush of relief that Eliza, at seven, was a whiz at first base and Jake, only four, had learned to slide like a pro. We were growing scented geraniums; we'd spent a week at the beach in Carpinteria; the diet he'd faxed me at the beginning of the summer was absolutely worthless.

Fred was working, I managed to get in, writing a movie for one of the networks. I didn't mention the phone call at the beginning of the summer, or the fence or the windows or my outsized lifestyle. I didn't mention that I'd borrowed the money from my mother and stepfather (no less disapproving, no less skeptical, they'd come through for me all the same). Still hedging my bets, still playing both ends against the middle, even as a grown woman with children of my own.

A swimming lesson, May, 1995. Crouching at the side of the pool, I reached in and did a little flutter kick with two fingers. The water was like a bathtub, thick as syrup, too warm for me, but the theory is that kids learn to swim easier if they're not thinking about how cold they are. Sure enough, my daughter, Eliza, who was four in the summer of '94, splashed across the width of the pool, face down, kicking out of rhythm but with total abandon, hands gripping the edge of a faded blue Styrofoam board.

My father sat behind me in a small triangle of shade, tipping back in a plastic chair at a table under a broken white umbrella, chewing, as always, the cuticle on the side of his thumb. Waiting.

I caught the teacher's eye, gestured back to the umbrella table with my chin. "Eddie," I said, "my father would like to buy your hat."

My father, silent as a foreign ambassador, nodded at Eddie, who was just a kid, bronzed, hairless, wearing long red trunks, a white T-shirt, dark glasses, and a monster sombrero with a leather string that went around the brim and dangled just below his collarbone. There was a frayed hole in the straw on the side, and the hat was graying like a cottage on the Cape from all that water and sun.

Eddie laughed at the joke and to my daughter, who had reached the other side of the pool and was blowing bubbles, he said, "One more time across, Eliza. Let me see your strokes, now, and you can dive for rings afterwards, okay?"

"Name your price," my father barked, fluent in English after all, tilting forward in his undersized seat.

Eddie said he needed his hat and couldn't possibly sell it.

"How much do you want?" My father spoke slowly, with as much patience as he could muster. His assistant, his staff, as it were (that was me), had failed him. He'd have to make the deal himself.

Eliza shouted at me to watch, and she bounced up and down not far from the steps, where the water reached only to her shoulders.

"I see you, sweetie," I said, squinting into the sun, then crossing away from the glare to stand in the little wedge of shade beside my father's umbrella table.

"C'mon, Eliza, show me one more lap," said Eddie, and when she pushed off from the side, arms flailing like a broken propeller, he told my father, "I'm sorry, sir, this hat is not for sale."

"That's right," I said, "you stick to your guns—don't give in—he thinks he can boss everybody around."

My father leaned back again, legs crossed. He was starting to have fun, I could tell.

"Name your price."

A woman sitting cross-legged on the cement on the other side of the pool looked up from the newspaper spread across her knees and stared at him. Suddenly embarrassed, I reminded him, my voice a little too loud, that Eddie needed his hat teaching lessons back to back under the midday sun.

There were two pools side by side on the flat expanse of lawn, two shimmering pools reflecting a cloudless sky. Beyond them the grass was brown, although the oleander grew thick and high along the fence between this yard and those of the neighbors on either side. Two teachers worked in each pool and all four of them wore the informal uniform: some kind of T-shirt over some sort of bathing suit, dark shades, and wide-brimmed headgear.

"You don't want this old hat," Eddie apologized. "It's got a hole in it, see? It's falling apart."

"It's priceless," my father replied. "It's a relic, for Christ's sake, they don't make them like that anymore."

Now he was confiding in the kid, talking up his golf game. Loved the sport, he said, suddenly expansive, but all that sun exposure was a problem. Just a few days ago a dermatologist had charged him an arm and a leg to burn some growths off his face. He stroked his cheek, feeling for the scab with his fingers.

"That's just the hat I need," he said.

The woman, who had a child in the other pool, shook her head almost imperceptibly, and looked back down at her paper.

"Dad, leave him alone," I said.

I needed the woman to know that in this case, the apple had nothing to do with the tree; I was as confounded by this vulgarity as she.

Eddie threw three rings, fluorescent pink, orange, and green, and Eliza half jumped, half dove from the steps, wriggling to the bottom to retrieve them.

"How much do you make an hour?" asked my father.

I winced, watching Eddie shrug, smile, pat the surface of the water with his palms.

"Tell you what. I'll give you fifty bucks for the hat."

Eddie's eyes widened. "Shoot," he gasped.

My father slowly extracted a new fifty-dollar bill from the thick wad in his money clip and put the rest back in his pocket.

"Here it is." He put the bill on the table without getting up. "Take it or leave it."

I was ready for the bill to blow off the table and into the pool, and I stuck my hands in my pockets.

"I'll take it," said Eddie, removing the hat.

My father looked at me and nodded in Eddie's direction. I started to laugh, bit my lip, took the money off the table, and walked it over to the kid, who handed me the hat in return.

"More rings?" Eliza squealed. "More rings, more rings, more rings!"

"Time's up," Eddie said, glancing at the clock on the wall of an old shed behind the far pool. He was folding the bill into a square the size of a postage stamp, promising her more rings next week. He held the green square in one fist just out of the water, and I wondered when he would get out of the pool and put it away. His hair was flat on his head, a color somewhere between brown and green, shiny like tinsel from all the chlorine.

I held up an oversized beach towel, and Eliza shimmied out of the pool and into my arms, smelling of bleach and baby shampoo and Coppertone and leaving a big, wet print where she had pressed her head against my cotton sweater. My father examined his new hat, stood up, and put it on.

"Whaddayathink?" he asked my daughter.

"It has a hole," she observed, and she led the way up the driveway to the street, pausing to search for roly-poly bugs in the flower bed at the back of the house, trailing her yellow terrycloth train across the gravel behind her.

The woman with the newspaper was staring again, and when my father met her eye, acknowledging her role in the conspiracy, she gave him a terse, little smile. On his way past her, he pulled a cherry tomato from the vine that straggled along the fence between the pools and the driveway and popped it into his mouth. "Ummm," he said to her over his shoulder, as he grabbed another for the car, "that's sweet."

6 | Still Missing

On the day Fred and I were married, May 31, 1986, a day when the air hung hot and heavy like some kind of damp, invisible curtain, I dressed at the last possible minute, lingering in my underwear on the third floor of the house where I grew up in Pelham, New York, long before my mother put in central air conditioning. The guests had begun to arrive, mostly family and old friends, mostly comfortable letting themselves in, announcing themselves, letting the screen doors slam behind them. Up three flights, I was doing battle with pantyhose, swearing at my narrow pumps, trying to negotiate fabric-covered buttons with swollen fingers, when the front doorbell rang.

Jill, my sister, sixteen years old, answered the door in a long, flowered dress with a wreath in her hair. As she told it later, an oddly familiar man waited on the stoop.

"I'm Dinah's father," he explained to the beautiful (oddly familiar?) girl on the other side of the screen.

"Come in," she greeted him, pushing open the door and reaching out to shake hands. "I'm Dinah's sister."

I try to reach my stepmother. She isn't taking calls.

My mother and my stepfather are on vacation in Europe; I call their children, my younger half siblings, with whom I was raised.

Joe, the eldest of the three, doesn't answer the phone.

"I don't know what to do," I sob when I reach Andy, the younger of my two brothers.

"I don't know what to do either," he moans in sympathy.

Jill, the baby, is equally stymied. I should call her, she urges, as soon as I know anything. Or even if I don't.

This, she says before she hangs up, is the kind of thing that happens to somebody else. Poor thing, in her case, somebody else just happens to be her sister.

My husband comes home with the children, who disappear into their rooms before I whisper to him what I know, what I don't.

I wait by the phone.

My sister calls the next morning to say it's all over the television.

The FBI, brought in because my father's car has crossed state lines twice according to the automatic toll taker, and perhaps, too, because my father was a political figure in the '70s, assigns an agent to interview me on the telephone. The disembodied, New York-inflected voice has some questions: Maybe my father had a secret life? Maybe he wanted to disappear?

What, they think he's sipping Smirnoff on some tropical isle?

I'm flattered to be asked, as if I knew anything about my father's life, secret or otherwise, and I answer with conviction. No, never, not my father, he would never, I tell the man on the phone. And I know I am right. I remember the random phone calls at odd hours of the day, to tell me a joke, to give me a tip, to order me to make him airplane reservations, he was on his way to see me. He wasn't a deserter, not this man whose pride in ownership, whose hold on his own never loosened, never gave.

I make the peanut butter sandwiches.

I take my son to preschool.

I pick up my daughter at gymnastics.

I know where I have to be and when and I am early for each appointment because I don't know what to do with myself in between. Outside Eliza's second grade classroom I sit on a long bench, chipping away at the orange paint with my fingernail, avoiding inquiry and concern in the eyes of the other parents who have heard whispers, rumors, who have gone on the Internet and looked up the headlines back East.

"Do you think he's dead?" I ask my husband after we turn off the lights at night, and again before we get up in the morning, and again in the middle of the day, seated at the kitchen table with a cold cup of tea.

Fred, who writes movies for television, is a student of murder and mayhem, violence in the heartland and the underbelly of life in the big city. One time, years ago, he came up from his office in a rumpled shirt and messy hair with a pencil behind his ear to ask our poor, unsuspecting piano tuner if there was anything in his bag that could be used as a weapon. Infinitely patient, he answers my question each time as though I hadn't already asked. He might be dead, Fred tells me, carefully. But he might not be, he adds. The more time goes by the more dour he becomes.

College friends call from pay phones adjacent to newsstands in Manhattan. Old acquaintances call from pay phones adjacent to newsstands in airports in Chicago and Cleveland and Dallas and Boston.

I call my stepmother—sit on hold for three minutes, out of breath, heart pounding, one eye twitching, staring at my toes—but it turns out she still isn't taking calls.

I go to a callback for a part on a new prime time show called

Cracker. It's a drama about a criminal psychologist, and I'm reading for the role of a mother whose son has drowned. It's easy to cry, and I feel like a fraud when the feedback comes in, something about my intelligence, my depth, my layered portrayal. No, no, I'm thinking, it's just that there's really something happening to me for a change.

Friends visit with bottles of wine, mangos, watermelon, organic red seedless grapes.

"He's dead," I whisper to one of them when she hugs me.

"When did you hear?" She pulls away to search my face.

"I just know," I say. "I just know."

"Drink Gatorade," she orders with authority. "Stress is dehydrating."

7 | Driving Lessons

I'm missing a chunk of my right calf. All right, not a chunk. But truly there's a sizable dent just above the back of my ankle and a matching scar all the way around the other side on the front of my shin. The old marks are pale, shiny, too smooth to the touch, but barely noticeable nearly twenty years later. Even so when I look down the back of my leg, I can't help but wonder at the size of that husky's jaws.

The Friday after New Year's, 1985, Fred and I drove north to visit my brother Joe at his farmhouse in upstate New York. There was plenty of snow on the ground when we woke up Saturday morning and a good fire burning in the potbellied stove. We were planning a dinner party for assorted friends and relatives and a trip to the grocery store was in order, but first Fred went out for a three-mile run. Then, not to be outdone, I decided I, too, wanted exercise and why we didn't just go together I honestly don't remember. Fred warned me before I left about a mean dog on a farm along the route.

"I can handle dogs," I scoffed.

When Fred tells the story he still insists it was the red down vest we both wore that morning; the mean dog, he argues, assumed that I was he, come back for more. But don't dogs operate straight from the nose? Haven't I even read somewhere that dogs are color-blind? Fred, my screenwriter, is devoted to plot: the dog would have had to have a logical reason to come after me. According to the rules and elements of a good story, this couldn't have been a random act of violence.

When I saw the dog barreling down the hill, I stopped. Which is what you're supposed to do. You run, a dog gives chase. You stand still, he's likely to pause, himself. Maybe he'll snarl at you, but chances are he'll do it from a distance. But this dog never hesitated. He came at me with a vengeance, grabbed onto me with his teeth and tussled my leg as though it was a branch, a trophy he could tear off and carry away. Then, suddenly, he looked me in the eye and froze. He actually seemed surprised. Abruptly he dropped the prize and loped back up the hill to his farm.

So there I was on a quiet road, a half a mile or so from my brother and my boyfriend, a hundred yards from a farmhouse with smoke curling up out of the chimney, blue-black in a slate sky. There I was, and when I screamed at the sight of my own blood running all over the snow, it was for a man who was three hundred miles and over two hours away, housed in a suburb of New York City and most definitely out of earshot. Dad, I cried, Dad, Dad, Dad, Dad, Dad.

I was twenty-eight years old and I wanted the person who I knew could restore sanity, good health, and calm. I wanted my stepfather.

My father taught me how to take a long, curving turn at fast speeds.

"Pull over," he ordered, somewhere along leafy Route 17 in Bergen County, the northern part of New Jersey, well away from the Hudson River and Route 4, lined with strip malls and factories and fast food. "Now look," he said, just a tad contemptuous, having traded seats with me, having adjusted his headrest and the radio, and having entered the highway all over again just before the curve in the road where I'd demonstrated my ignorance.

"You don't pull to the right in one big jerk, see, you take it in increments like so," and one-handed, he pulled and released, pulled and released, making the turn in a smooth arc, never mind the staggered, staccato movements at the wheel.

My father and the car, the car and my father. He always drove a silver or midnight blue BMW, all leather interior and a car phone way before anybody else had one. My father loved to drive. He loved his car. He wasn't voluble about it but you could tell he was comfortable there. He had the seat just so, pushed back from the pedals to accommodate his large frame and he kept the radio tuned to Frank Sinatra or Howard Stern—Big Band music or all-talk-all-the-time—the ultimate entertainment being the O.J. trial. Really, I never heard him so excited. I would pick up my landlocked extension from the table behind the easy chair in my living room to hear the traffic three thousand miles away on the George Washington Bridge, and my father would shout, "Are you listening to this? Jesus Christ, how can you not be listening to this?"

My first car in LA was a Dodge, a stick shift, inherited from my father-in-law; a stripper, they called it at the dealership when we tried to sell it back, flat yellow with a spongy mustard interior, two doors, no air and roll-down windows. The next was a Ford Taurus, a hand-me-down from back East, four doors and a cooling system, thank God, no more red-faced infants squeezed into car seats from impossible angles causing permanent damage to middle-aged rotator cuffs. Then, finally, for my birthday, my father gave us the down payment for a lease on a new model, urging me to get a mini-van or a nice Japanese sedan, but I had to have my SUV first time out, a

Ford Explorer, and he enjoyed it, too, during his visits, when he borrowed it to tool over to Bel Air for a bit of golf.

He'd approve now, I think, of my Honda Odyssey; not fancy, but it seats seven on carpool days and parks in compact spaces. Plus, I own it outright, paid for it in full with money I inherited from my grandfather, his father. Money I never would have seen had he been alive when his own father died.

I don't have to close my eyes to conjure my father. I build him in parts, and I start with his cheek, the right one if *he's* driving, the left if *I'm* at the wheel. I can almost touch it, shockingly soft, fresh-shaved, one cheek or the other, sinking into jowl. From there, he comes into focus: Slavic eyes, heavy-lidded, bushy brows, the stray hairs seem to catch in his lashes, receding hairline but not very gray, a big face, a big head, a smirk or no expression at all. He's indifferent to me mostly, or distracted by something out the window, until I jolt him with a joke, an opinion; then he's reluctantly amused, chuckles, maybe, yeses me, but the truth is, I seldom know what he's really thinking.

On the road we were easy with each other, my father and I. First off, we were used to it; picking each other up, dropping each other off, chauffeuring and being chauffeured. Then, too, there was all that white noise, and the fact that it was perfectly acceptable, in transit, not to look a person in the eye when speaking or listening or not talking at all.

My father taught me to take a long curve. But it was Ron, my stepfather, who taught me how to drive in a Ford Country Squire in the fall of 1972, in the parking lot of Huguenot Church across from Four Corners and up and down the Esplanade, the street where we lived. When I stood at the end of the big bed in the middle of the night after a bad dream, Ron was the one who opened his eyes, told me to get a drink of water and go back to bed. It was Ron who moved me in and out of a half a dozen apartments from the time I left for college until I moved to California almost a decade later, and it's he whom my children have called *Grandpa* from the time that they could say the word. I can't say how strange and right it was that my stepfather held me to him on the afternoon of my father's memorial service, when I stopped to see him on my way to Kennedy Airport and back to Los Angeles.

"How you doing, Babe?" he asked me.

"Not so good," I answered.

"No," he said, "there's nothing good about this."

8 | Waiting

"Officials were tight-lipped about what they think happened to Gross, a real estate developer and restaurateur whose wife is the chairwoman of the New Jersey Racing Commission and who himself was a fixture in local and state politics during the 1970s.

The FBI yesterday joined the Bergen County Prosecutor's Office in the investigation, though officials of neither agency would say much except that they are treating the incident as a suspected kidnapping.

. . . In addition to his wife Noel and his son Neil, Gross has a daughter who lives in California."

The Star Ledger, Saturday, September 20, 1997

He's been missing for two days, and I wonder what to tell my children.

The first child psychologist (where did I find her?) says we must tell them their grandfather is missing and promise we will never get lost.

The second child psychologist explains that the truth is important, we must explain that this situation is unusual, and assure them we are doing everything we can to find "Grandpa."

I tell my children nothing. I lie sideways across the bed with a pillow over my head and the cordless phone beside me.

"Do you hope he's dead?" I ask my uncle's wife.

"Of course not," she scolds.

But it's been three days, four days, five days, better dead than suffering, yes? Better dead than locked in a cellar somewhere. Better dead than buried alive in a hole in the ground.

The police find his car, with one broken window, in a bleak neighborhood in Washington Heights.

I call my uncle who tells me to sit tight, not to travel, no reason to come, there's nothing I can do.

I call my stepmother who simply cannot talk to me at this time.

I read the newspapers.

My husband gets me a prescription for sleeping pills.

The third child psychologist counsels in a lilting accent like a sad Italian song; she is so very sorry, this is so terrible, I must be longing to tell my children, longing for their comfort, but it is my responsibility to protect them from such a horror as this.

My husband is relieved. He drives the carpool, orders the pizza. *He* makes the peanut butter sandwiches. I read more headlines, I watch more television. Deep in the night after the kids are long asleep, I visit them in their beds, press my nose into their warm little necks, inhale their hot, sweet-and-sour snores, resolve to control myself when they are awake so as to be able to keep my silence, so as not to have to justify bad behavior.

I leave a message for my mother and Ron in a hotel in Europe.

"Nelson is missing," I tell my other father when he calls me back.

"What?"

"My father has disappeared. He took twenty thousand dollars out of the bank and drove off in his car with a couple of strangers."

"Hold on, I'll get Mom," Ron says.

Moments pass and the alarm in her voice is palpable when she picks up the extension.

"How can he be missing?" she asks.

"I don't know," I say, starting to cry. "It's all over the television."

"Do you need us to come home?"

But I know that she's due back in New York in just a few days, and I promise her there's nothing she can do for me. It's just that I didn't want her to hear about it on the news or from somebody else. It's just that I needed so badly to hear her voice.

I get a part on *Cracker*, but not the one I'd read for at the audition, in spite of my authentic tears.

I call my stepmother who is indisposed.

I go to an afternoon concert in the park. I wear a pale yellow dress that hangs down to my ankles but blows up around my waist at the least provocation. People lie on their backs with their arms crossed under their heads and a section of the Sunday *Times* folded over their faces. Children hop from rock to rock in a dry creek and have to be constantly hushed and the orchestra crescendos, swells with the breeze and pushes the clouds across the sky. I can't sit in one place. I stand holding my dress to my sides, waiting. Just waiting. I know it is raining, raining day after day, in New York.

Neil, my half brother with his own tarnished history (substance abuse, academic probation, that sort of thing), is interrogated. Turns out he found my father's wallet on the office floor the morning of the disappearance and kept it to himself for twenty-four hours before handing it over to the authorities.

Thinking he has to know something, the police rough him up a little, leaving him furious and humiliated. Then—according to the family grapevine—a bouncer from the restaurant, devoted to both father and son, takes it upon himself to throw a punch or two, as if he could accomplish what law enforcement can't. Bruised and beaten now, inside and out, Neil is as baffled as the rest of us—he has nothing to tell.

"What if we never find him?" I whisper to Fred in the middle of the night. "What if we never find out what happened?"

I hardly know who I am anymore. I am following my physical self through the moves, like an extra shadow. I am trying to catch up to my life.

And I am waiting.

9 | My Old Man

I wore a plaid jumper and big, flat Capezios when I went to Trenton on election night in 1972. Enamel ladybugs dangled from my ears on tiny gold wires. This was an occasion, and I was staying over with my grandparents in Englewood and missing school the next day.

Campaign headquarters was in the banquet hall of an enormous hotel. Upstairs, my grandmother, sturdy and unstoppable, pushed me through the cigarette smoke and the crowd to where my grandfather drank scotch in a leather club chair directly in front of one of half a dozen blaring televisions. I perched on the arm of the chair, as close to him as I could.

"I'm going to put diamonds in those ears," he told me.

I fished an ice cube out of his glass and put it in my mouth.

"Don't chew ice cubes, Dinah dear," said my grandmother.

"Leave her alone, she's gorgeous," said my grandfather.

My grandmother agreed I was perfect and pushed me, gently, from the arm of the chair. "Say hello to your daddy, darling."

My father, deep in conversation, looked just like the picture on the button pinned to my blouse, on the posters on every wall, on the banner hung across the far bay window, on the billboard on the Jersey side of the George Washington Bridge. Noel stood beside him with her arm around Neil, in short pants and suspenders, and across from the governor of New Jersey, whose campaign my father had successfully managed two years before.

"This is one of Nelson's young supporters," she explained, unable to pretend I wasn't standing at her elbow.

"Lovely to meet you, young lady," said the governor. "You look just like your dad, don't you?"

When my father saw me he put his hand on my shoulder and steered me to the bar. "This is my daughter," he said to the bartender, and "Say hello to my daughter," to a burly man with a cigar in his mouth, who leaned over to whisper something in his ear.

"Good to meet you, honey," said the man. "I hope you know your father's going to be the vice president of this country one of these days."

My father laughed and ordered me a Shirley Temple with two cherries. I didn't tell him I'd hated maraschino cherries ever since that time in the fourth grade when I'd eaten a whole jar of them and consequently thrown up.

For the concession speech, Paul stood me up on a chair in the back of the banquet hall so I could see. I was in love with my father then, handsome, benevolent, extending himself to the crowd and praising his staff.

Afterward, back in the hotel suite, the carpets were littered with crumpled cocktail napkins and toothpicks and cigarette ash and water stains, and the televisions were silent as tombstones. I only had to retrieve my duffel coat and say good-bye to my father, whose eyes were bloodshot and tired.

"Gee, Dine, I'm sorry," he said when he hugged me. "I hope you're not too disappointed in your old man."

I squeezed by a uniformed woman and her vacuum cleaner to catch up with my grandparents in front of the elevator. *My old man?* But my father wasn't even forty in the fall of 1972.

Uncle Paul offers a one hundred thousand dollar reward for safe return. Then he offers twenty-five thousand dollars for information leading to arrest and conviction. A street informant comes forward. In exchange for the money he tells the cops that three punks in the neighborhood are bragging about doing *some old man.* They're showing off new jewelry, new clothes, fancy hubcaps, and a used motorcycle, but it's in real good shape.

I was startled, I remember, when my father referred to himself as my *old man* in 1972. My old man? Who was that? Sometimes on television a punk teenager called his father *my old man.* Joni Mitchell, my vocal hero, sang a song about her *old man,* but he was her lover, wasn't he? It had never occurred to me to call either of my fathers *old man,* and I found this stab at the vernacular, at nonchalance under duress, embarrassing and awkward. Who was this person who thought I could ever call him such a thing?

Some old man.

In 1989 my father followed me in his rental car to a local restaurant, missed the turn into the parking lot, and did a U-ey in the middle of the avenue.

"Fuck you, old man!" screamed the driver behind him, brandishing his forefinger like a machine gun out the window as he screeched past us and through a yellow light a hundred yards or so ahead.

Moments later I watched my father hoist his strapping self up out of the car. He was fifty-seven then—gray at the temples, but tall, broad-shouldered, fit—and I was more outraged than he at the insult. (Had he even heard it? Did he ignore it to preserve his dignity or had he missed the slur altogether?) How dare that asshole call him old, how dare he?

Some *old man*. *My* old man. Sixty-five. Eligible for a senior citizen discount at the movies and a social security check. Missing, presumably dead, for the sake of new hubcaps.

10 | The House with the Gate

ME: I got all As, Dad, are you proud of me?

I hate camp. I love pickles. I never drink milk.

I'm the lead in the play!

Look, I have a retainer. No, I don't smoke cigarettes.

Do you like my hair?

I got asked to the prom!

Did you see me on TV?

Tell me, Dad, what do you think about Nixon, Reagan, Clinton, the Unabomber, earthquakes, the house market, the job market, the farmer's market?

HIM: Good news, Dine. Good for you.

Sorry about that.

Glad to hear that.

Good.

Good.

Looks good.

Good.

Saw that show. You were good.

A crook, a hero, a fool, a nutcase.

Don't I keep saying? Get a regular job, stay out of stocks,

put your money in real estate, and pick up some decent tomatoes, will you, I'll wait in the car.

"So, Dad, I send you all these clippings, and you don't say a
word."

I was giving him a tour of Hancock Park. He'd come to stay
with us for a few days maybe six miles to the east, where we
still live in the hills just west of Dodger Stadium. Back then,
before the gentrification of Echo Park, there was seldom a Saturday night when we didn't fall asleep to salsa and Mariachi
rhythms and a symphony of howling dogs. There were roost-
ers in the valley below, and some anonymous guy kept goats
and pigs behind a hedge of bamboo in a vacant lot opposite
Magic Gas on Echo Park Avenue. The billboards advertising
pediatric dentistry and Coca-Cola were all in Spanish and there
was a Burrito King on every corner. Our neighbor to the north
was Elizabeth—benign but surly—and her white hair floated
and waved in the breeze like cobwebs. She reminded us often
how she tolerated our trash cans, all three of them placed to
one side of our driveway, on the edge of her property. Frank,
who still lives next door on the other side, was—still is—a ward
of the state. A clothesline stretched across his front door. From
the street you could see newspapers piled high against his windows and the blue light of the television, day in, day out. From
the deck off our kitchen, we could watch his satellite dish in
the corner of his overgrown backyard, buzzing and shifting
like something alive.

My father had wondered aloud if we were safe here, and I
demurred, only vaguely ashamed, because I saw his query as a
kind of opportunity. Would he like to see a different neighborhood? Yes, he would. So there we were, driving past enormous
houses built within a few feet of their half-acre lots, so close
together the residents could peer over each others' driveways
and into each others' state-of-the-art bathrooms every time

they brushed their teeth. Brick Tudors with turrets and tiled haciendas with interior courtyards; perfect houses with perfect lawns and shiny four-wheel-drive vehicles in tasteful colors, eggplant or sage, mauve or slate blue, parked in those driveways as wide and winding as little rivers. I took him through the neighborhood as though I was an insider and as if my good taste alone deserved a down payment.

When I was little, my father promised to buy me a pony. When I learned to drive, he said he would get me a car. I'd long since forgiven him for not coming through; still, I felt he owed me. Here and now was my moment: maybe he'd make it all up to me and buy me a house!

"I like that one," he said, pointing out the window to a square of pink stucco just visible beyond a tall, vine-covered wrought iron fence. "I like that gate. Makes it private, secure, you can't see a thing on the other side."

It was hideous, an ostentatious prison on a busy corner, and I stuck out my tongue and told him so. My father and I had never been able to impress each other in matters of taste; he had no appreciation for my good manners, and I had always marveled at just how tacky he could be. The difference between us was that I cared—I continued to try to impress him—while he, easy in his skin, remained oblivious to my gymnastics. This time I was standing on my head about my column in a local parent magazine; I'd been sending him the pieces as they were published, and I wanted him to tell me how clever they were.

"I'm telling you, Dinah," he said, looking back at it as we rounded the corner, "*that's* a good house."

"What about my clippings, Dad?" I asked again.

"What clippings?" he spat out the window, and when I reminded him about the envelope I'd mailed just a few weeks before, he shrugged, pulled on the end of his nose, and told me the piece was not his "kind of thing."

How to stop myself from keeping score? He'd never heard me play "Clair de Lune"; he'd never asked to see a single report card; he'd missed the high school production of *Auntie Mame*. I'm the singer on that jazz tape he misplaced before he got around to listening; I'm the daughter from the first marriage, accepted to his alma mater straight out of public school, tapped freshman year to swim long distance for the varsity team, and he never once came to a meet.

What I wanted was for him to admit I was exceptional, before mediocrity—in the guise of motherhood and bit parts on television—completely took over my life. So I continued to press, which I knew, on some level, was futile, not to mention pathetic.

"The writing is fine," he conceded at last. "The writing is intelligent, but it's not my kind of thing, that's all." He took up every inch of space on the passenger side, legs splayed wide, one arm flung across the back of the seat, the other elbow leaning on the open window, his feet, size 12, resting on either bank of the well beneath him.

"It's not your kind of thing," I repeated, sneering at myself in the rearview mirror, but my bitterness went unacknowledged. The real estate, it turned out, was too compelling.

"There's another good house," he said, pointing to a spanking new Georgian with lots of pillars and a huge crystal chandelier, visible from the street, "but it's not secure, that one, doesn't have a gate."

"Dad, whose kind of thing do you think it is, huh?"

Why couldn't I stop?

"Gee, I don't know." He knit his brow, pretending to try to figure it out.

I told him my grandfather, his father, thought the columns, each of them under seven hundred words, were "very chatty." He agreed this was apt.

"Dad, did you even read them?" I asked. "Did you?"

A confrontation, I must have supposed, would be better than nothing. How to rattle him, how to get a response, how to make him know me, and, come to think of it, who the hell was this guy sitting beside me in the passenger seat? My father looked at me hard, eyebrows drawn together, and then back out the window. He inhaled, held his breath just a moment, then exhaled through his nose.

"I think," he said, slow and measured, pulling on the end of his nose, "I think you should stay in the house you're in. It works for you."

Okay then. He wasn't going to bite. No pony, no Pinto—Ford or otherwise—and no partial down payment on a house in the offing either.

"I need a guest bedroom," I moaned. "I need more space."

"What do you need a guest bedroom for? You don't want guests. What do you need guests for?"

Present company excepted, presumably, since that time two or three visits back, when he'd called from the Downtown Hilton before seven o'clock in the morning to say he'd like to have breakfast at our house, I should pick him up *now*. When I got there, he was waiting in the lobby with his bags and his golf clubs, having checked out because he'd decided it'd be more convenient for everybody if he stayed with us. During subsequent visits, he'd been happier than I could have imagined in my son's single bed, which faces the driveway and gets very little natural light. And the truth was, I was flattered, pleased that he was comfortable enough with us to stay for a few days, to let me cook for him, make his bed, wash his clothes. I was appalled at his helplessness but eager to wait on him, this stranger, who left the bedclothes in a heap, smeared the shaving cream across the counter, missed the bowl when he peed. This was my opportunity to prove myself a good and capable daughter.

But could it be he believed he wasn't *company*? I tried not to frown, explaining that guests or no, we were squished in our house. A playroom would be nice, a flat yard for the kids, a wide street with a sidewalk for an evening stroll or a chance meeting with neighbors who also had children.

"Flat is better," he agreed. "I'm not crazy about those hills."

Stupid, stupid me. I'd opened up a whole other subject. He was reminding me now that he'd never have advised us to buy in Echo Park. Location, location, he chided, like a realtor, and then he added, back on task, "But for God's sake, stay where you are, you don't need to invest any more money in Los Angeles. This flat part is fine, but it could all burn down in some riot next week."

He massaged his golf arm.

"I'll tell you what, Dinah," he blurted into the silence, "I couldn't do it, that's for sure. I could never do that kind of thing. Never."

"What?"

He'd taken a writing course his freshman year at Yale, did I know? I was incredulous. He'd wanted to write?

"Write!" he sneered. "Are you kidding? I heard it was easy. An easy credit. I didn't know I had to turn in something every class."

"Daily themes!"

"That's right, that's it. Daily Themes. They said it was a, a whaddayacallit—"

"A *gut*."

He nodded with emphasis, and I was inordinately proud that I'd filled in the right word.

"Yup. I signed up for this *gut* and then I couldn't do it. I was stuck."

He explained that my grandfather did the work for him, mailed him the themes at the beginning of each week. My brilliant grandfather, a criminal attorney, an artist, a musician, a hero as far as I was concerned, and this new information was unnerving. I was, after all, the straight arrow kid, ever righteous, a veritable moral compass, if only they knew what a good egg I was. If only they cared. Why did I expect my father to respond to anything I'd achieved? And on the other hand, why didn't he regard me as something of a miracle? And why, oh why, wouldn't he tell me so?

We were below Olympic Boulevard now and the lots were smaller, burnt-out lawns, tangled sunflowers, bougainvillea climbing over chicken wire, a pickup with no front wheels in one driveway and scrawny trees coming up from the pavement.

I took a breath. "Well, they must have been beautiful, huh? Grandpa's themes?"

My father shrugged. He remarked, as we passed a horde of kids running through a revolving sprinkler in a driveway, that this was a terrible neighborhood. How could anyone live here is what he wanted to know.

I asked him if he got an A in Daily Themes.

"Nah, I got a B. The bastard knew something was up. He knew I couldn't be doing the work." My father quit massaging his arm and chewed a cuticle on the side of his thumb.

I was still shaking my head over my grandfather's having bailed him out, and I wondered out loud why he did it. The light turned green and somebody honked behind me.

"He knew I couldn't do it, Dinah. That's all."

Gee. No scruples. No honor. No cheerleading, no slap on the wrist, no nothing. Just get it done however you can.

I was winding my way north again, up a street shaded under long rows of gnarled California oaks.

"I'll tell you something else, but if you ever tell another soul, I'll deny it," he warned with a squint in my direction.

He confided then that he'd taken my half brother's final exams to ensure Neil's graduating with his college class. I was stunned. Wasn't that illegal? How could he do such a thing? How'd he get away with it?

My father said he knew Neil couldn't pass. It was easy enough; he showed up with a couple of No. 2 pencils, that was all. He warned me again to keep the information to myself.

I pretended amusement, but I was writhing inside. The man was willing to lie and cheat, he was willing to be lied and cheated for. So what was a little approval, I wondered—a compliment or two, and some money for a down payment—between father and daughter. In the grand scheme of things, I hadn't asked for much. I'd followed the rules. I was a credit to this guy. I was the best thing about him, wasn't I?

"Hey, now, this one is very attractive," he said, pointing out the window, "but you can't afford to live here, can you?" He was staring out at what looked like a mini-Parthenon on the opposite corner. "You've been telling me what's wrong with your house since you moved in, but it seems fine to me."

"Okay, okay. It's fine. We're fine, we are."

"I'm hungry," said my father. "It must be time for lunch."

"Listen, Dad," I said, gripping the wheel hard with both hands, "I know you think I'm a fool."

He stared at me, quizzical, wounded even. He hated heart-to-heart stuff, always had.

"Remember?" I asked. "When I left the job at the restaurant to do stock at the Weathervane? You said," I dropped my voice an octave, "'You're a fool, whatsamatterwithyou, you're a fool.'"

He'd been sitting in an overstuffed armchair ten years before, perfectly cheerful, with a drink in one hand, when I, quaking in my shoes, turned down his offer of full-time employment at the restaurant for a summer of nonunion stock. I'd cried as I told him, and he'd laughed at me, actually guffawed, disgusted with my tears.

"You probably think I should just go out and get some civilian job, sell insurance, work in a bank, just get on with it, right?" Couldn't help myself, couldn't keep from baiting him, could have done with a roll of duct tape at that point, no question.

"Hey, Dinah, don't ask, you've never listened to me, you've never done anything I told you to do your whole life."

Now wasn't this what I wanted all the time? Not approval, no, I wanted a strong reprimand: I wasn't a good girl after all, I couldn't afford to live in a nice neighborhood, my acting career stuttered at best, I wrote dumb pieces for a dumb magazine, and I had never listened to my father. Here came the tears, the easy tears, and they were humiliating. At a stop sign, I blinked hard behind my sunglasses.

My father started to chuckle.

I swallowed and asked him what was so funny.

"Did you hear what I said? *You've never listened to me.* . . . Christ, my father said the same thing to me," he gasped, "the very same thing."

"He did? Really? When? When did he say it?"

"Last week," my father was wiping his eyes. "He said it last week."

"And look how well you've turned out since, right?" I was appropriately grateful, relieved to be in on the joke.

"I guess so," he nodded, serious now, looking me straight in the eye.

His face was my own, a near-mirror reflection, but who was he really, and what was he thinking, what did he see in me with those almond-shaped eyes? We were the same and we were absolute strangers, my father and I, and he liked it that way. It was acceptable; it was the best he could offer. Could it be he believed we were close?

"You know, Dad," I offered, "one of these days I might write a book."

He regarded me soberly.

"Uh oh," he said.

And then his face cracked wide in a smile, broad across the cheeks, both eyes crinkling in my direction. Because he didn't care? Because he didn't think I had it in me? Either way I couldn't help but laugh back, grateful to know he appreciated the implications whether he believed me or not. We chuckled in collusion, connected for an instant by some strange conspiracy of genealogy and temperament.

The neighborhood tour was complete. We'd come full circle at the corner of Rossmore and Beverly. I put on my blinker and eased into the right lane, pointing us back to Echo Park. My father's attention was focused once more out the window, where the Spanish stucco manse the color of Pepto-Bismol loomed beyond a tall tangle of ivy and iron.

"Hey look, there it is!" he said, pointing in delight. "I'm telling you, Dinah, *that's* a good house. Secure, private. Can't see anything behind that gate."

11 | I Remember

Jake looks sideways at me, then addresses my friend, who is sitting at the counter waiting for the demonstration.

"I'll show you."

He sticks out his brown, dimpled hand, creased with grime, streaked purple with marker, sand in his fingernails.

"Pop taught me this handshake," he says, and he sneaks a peek from under his lashes to make certain I've heard him and that I'm pleased.

He doesn't really remember, but he's been well-rehearsed. I've created this memory for him. I've told him how my father made him practice shaking hands firmly, clapped him on the back, and roared with pleasure when he got it right.

Here's what I remember:

My father, swearing over my ski boots, buckling me up with those trembling fingers. Hoisting my skis onto his shoulders and walking ahead of me to the bottom of the lift, snapping me into my bindings and pushing me into the line.

My father in starched shirttails, crisp, white boxers, shiny, flat shoes, and garters just under his kneecaps attached to silky black socks.

My father schooling me on the tennis court in the heat of July: "This isn't ballet! Bend your knees, bend your knees!" he shouts in frustration.

My father swimming laps at dusk, leaning on his left arm just a little too long when he turns his head to breathe.

My father crossing and uncrossing his legs in the aisle seat of a Broadway musical, which we leave well before the curtain call, because he cannot bear the crowds bottlenecking toward the exit signs at the end of a show.

My father, trimming the cypress trees next to the swimming pool the day after he's lost the election to the U.S. Senate. When I tell my mother, she picks up the kitchen wall phone and calls him. "You're a mensch, Nellie," she says, red-nosed, handkerchief clenched between her fingers. It's his work ethic that gets to her, the idea of his doing chores in the face of failure (never mind that I never saw him with clippers in his hands before or afterward). It's the only time I can remember their having a conversation in all of my fifteen years; I stand in the mud room, on the other side of the wall, pretending not to listen, unable to breathe for a moment, even after she hangs up.

My father on the deck of his yacht, hosting a party two nights before I am to be married.

My father—a guest on my wedding day—a guest, but different, asserting his presence, demanding his due. After the ceremony, he takes me by the shoulders and turns me to him, saying, in a choked sort of voice, that I look "just beautiful." Later he leads me to the dance floor. I don't know how to follow—I'm hopeless—but he doesn't seem to notice really.

My father and I walking the beach in South Hampton where high tide has formed an inland swimming hole, and where my baby daughter toddles along beside him, slipping from the sand into the bog, way over her head. He reaches in and pulls her out, and I feel, somehow, he has saved my life.

My father, playing sports announcer, judging the progress of a snail race up the stucco behind our table in an outdoor café on LA's East Side.

My father scratching his Jack Russell, Jimmy, behind the ears.

My father slumped over the table, or leaning back in his chair; he spreads himself over surfaces, spills out over edges, like syrup on the countertop he cannot be contained.

My father stealing menus from local restaurants, growing tomatoes as big as cabbages in his vegetable garden, eating cold mashed potatoes straight from the fridge.

My father lying prone on my coffee table, lifting weights and grunting in perfect syncopation.

My father running up the trail, ahead of me at the curve, disappearing behind a hill covered with mustard flowers.

My father bribing my daughter with a jar full of nickels to hurdle all the jumps in the paddock behind the barn, and when she does, he laughs and laughs, wiping the corners of his slanting brown eyes.

My father pitching pennies for my children in my living room.

My father, putting into the ocean, swearing at the little white ball.

My father taking panoramic pictures while my children run circles around each other on the sand beside the water.

My father, teaching my son to shake hands with a firm grip.

12 | Albert and Rose

My grandfather outlived my father by six months, leaving Paul and Michael to argue over how to explain Nelson's absence.

Paul saw no reason to agitate the old man. As things were, he was demented and miserable, waiting to die. Why upset him further? Michael, on the other hand, was uncomfortable with pretending. This wasn't information that they could rightfully withhold, besides which, my grandfather would expect Nelson's daily visits that winter, would ask where he was and why he hadn't been in touch.

"This was his son," Michael insisted. "He deserves to know the truth. Wouldn't you want the truth?"

In the end Michael took the telling into his own hands. He flew to Florida with the news that my father was dead of a heart attack. What was the point of telling the truth when it wasn't the truth at all? Still, I was relieved somehow that my grandfather knew. Stuck on the opposite coast, estranged by this time from most of my father's family, lonely in grief, I wanted to be able to speak with my grandfather, to comfort him and for him to comfort me.

But it seems to me now that afterward, after he heard, he

pretty much stopped speaking altogether. If I was able to get him on the telephone neither of us mentioned my father. Albert had disappeared into senility or else he hadn't the strength, the desire, to pretend to make sense of anything anymore. The old man didn't know his eldest wouldn't ever be an old man. His nurse Eva, a large, beaming person, deep-voiced and Mediterranean, assured me he'd been told. He'd simply forgotten. When I tried again several weeks later, desperate for a real exchange, Eva said, "Oh Dinah, my dear, he's hollering today." She explained they were exercising his arms and legs, my call would cheer him, she said, and in spite of my protests, she put the phone against his ear.

"Grandpa," I asked him, "how are you?"

"Lousy," he shouted. "I'm lousy," he wailed, and I was stunned by the power in his voice, the power and the despair, almost operatic; it was not at all the sort of voice you'd expect from an invalid, a broken old man who hadn't left his bed in weeks.

"They're hurting my arms."

"Did you tell them to stop?"

"Yes, but they won't. I wish you'd tell them," he whimpered.

"Oh Grandpa, I love you, I wish you felt better."

"Eva," he cried, "Eeeevaaaaa." On his end, the phone clattered to the floor.

"Eva?" I yelled as though she could hear me from the other side of his sickroom. "Eva, are you there?"

More shouting. Swearing. "Eva, for fuck's sakes," bellowed my erudite grandfather from his bed.

I was on my feet then, trembling, about to hang up when Eva finally came back to the extension.

"Yes, honey, yes, honey," she soothed Albert. "Don't worry, Dinah, he's doing good."

"I'm doing good, I'm doing good, she's breaking my fucking arm," shouted my grandfather.

"Try another day," Eva suggested. "Today, my dear, your grandpa is hollering."

I never spoke to my grandfather again; never saw him either, it turned out, except dressed in white, painted like a mannequin, face-up in a coffin.

"I thought you should see," Michael said before the funeral, opening the box for my cousins and me. "You know how unhappy he was all these months, and now he looks so peaceful, don't you think?"

I thought he looked swollen and oddly small, confined in the box, no way to roll over, blown-up like a monster beach toy and not like anyone I ever knew.

But he'd lived ninety long, rewarding years; sad as death always is, my grandfather's was timely, sensible, an opportunity to celebrate his life. The terrible thing was to fly to New Jersey, to attend my second funeral in just over six months; to wear the same green suit and the same green earrings, my father's tie pin clipped to my belt loop this time, to be milling around with all those people I only ever saw because I am Nelson's daughter, and Nelson nowhere to be found. He wasn't anywhere in or out of the room so he had to be dead. How else could he not be standing up at his own father's funeral?

We fall into camps in this family: we are like Albert, my father's father, Harvard-educated, the violinist, the sculptor, the thinker, the writer, the speaker (the summer I graduated from college, I wrote my grandparents a long letter about my most keenly felt convictions and aspirations, and it was he who replied: *Dinah dear, Your Grandmother has been so completely devastated by the scope and content of your letter that the task, pleasant to be sure, of replying has been delegated to me)*; or we are like

Rose, unable to articulate our feelings even as they well up and trickle out the corners of our Mongolian eyes.

Fred and Albert used to sit on the deck off our kitchen in Los Angeles and play chess all afternoon. From his rocking chair Grandpa would survey the property and offer up house and gardening tips.

"My darling," he said once, "you must move this elegant yellow rose, the pot is too heavy for this uppermost deck."

And, peering out over the railing on the garden below, "Here's what you must do, Dinah, darling, spray the fungus off that cactus with a good, strong hose."

When he wasn't dispensing advice, Grandpa told jokes and stories, admired Fred's piles of jazz tapes and my piles of cookbooks, while Rose, my grandmother, weeded the clover out of the potted plants and pruned the geraniums that bordered the steps down to the bottom of the backyard.

The last time Fred played chess with Albert we were visiting back East and stopped in for a reunion at Paul's house in Hillsdale. At my grandmother's urging, Fred set up the board on a table under a tree, and he and Albert sat down to play. Five minutes later my grandfather was out of the chair, trudging up the slope of the yard towards the house, shooing us away without meeting our eyes, muttering, loud enough for us to hear, about how, having nothing in the least to do with his vision, he couldn't *see* the board anymore, it just wasn't any use.

He was tired of giving advice. My father and his brothers went to Albert about a business deal around that time. The story goes that he stared at them in disbelief, his deadpan delivery not intended to cover his exasperation. "Boys," he said, "it's time you got yourselves another advisor."

Old age isn't fair; it's sad and senseless and loaded with irony and, no way around it, my grandmother shouldn't have been the first to die. Albert was the old one. Albert was feeble and tired. Rose, relentlessly chipper, scolded and harangued him out of despondency and fatigue right up until the day she had the stroke that killed her in a week's time.

Without Rose around to egg him on, Albert all but gave up. Or gave in, I should say, to dementia and round the clock care in a condominium in Florida where his sons checked on him from time to time, my father most frequently, because he wintered nearby with his wife and her stable of thoroughbreds. Once, the story goes, when Michael was visiting, he decided to give his father a real treat. With much planning and enlisted manpower, Michael lifted Grandpa from his bed to his chair, wheeled the chair on to the specially equipped van, and set off for the ocean, driver and nurse in tow. He timed the trip so that the sun, bright and high in a cloudless sky, was just beginning its descent as they pulled off the road and parked above the beach. All by himself, Michael wheeled his father out onto a flat rock ledge that looked out over the Atlantic, wide and glinting, so endlessly blue, you could barely see where the water met the sky. The sun must have been dropping quickly by then, red in a canvas streaked with orange and violet, I imagine, and the two of them sat side by side, the perfect quiet punctuated only by the occasional cawing of the gulls and the breaking of surf on the shore. Only father and son and this view—all things universal and eternal throbbing in the silence—and Michael must have felt in the moment that he'd done something good and essential.

Eventually Grandpa cleared his throat, suddenly and obviously impatient. His voice, shaky and old, and still unmistakably tinged with Boston, with Harvard, rang out with the prosecutor's pointed eloquence.

"What," he asked in Michael's general direction, "*what* can be taking the waiter so long?"

We called her Rosie when we were waxing wise, being *fresh*. Otherwise it was Grandma, or Granny, or Gram.

Rose was the eldest of five, four girls and a boy, born to Barney and Celia Nelson, raised in a big, brick house in Leonia, New Jersey. Barney was a Russian Jew who'd emigrated in the early part of the century and made a fortune in construction.

A mutual friend, a college classmate of Albert's, set him up with one of the other Nelson girls over a long weekend. When Florence, her younger sister, neglected to show for tennis that Saturday morning, Rose took her place. Grandpa dismissed this recollection with a wave of his hand. "I only remember," he always said, "your grandmother's smile.

"When she opened the door with that smile of hers, she captivated me." He went on as though she were a fictional character and not the woman standing on the other side of the kitchen, urging someone to have another piece of roast chicken, please.

"Albert," she might have said at that point, patting his shoulder, "I have honeydew in the fridge."

"I don't want it," my grandfather would have grumbled in retort, hunched over in his chair at the dining table.

Undeterred, Rose would have cut a wedge of melon and placed it down in front of him, admonishing him to sit up straight on her way back to the sink with his dinner plate.

And Grandpa would have pushed it away. "Rose, I told you I don't want that," he'd have snapped, and then dropping all irritation, "As simple as that, she captivated me, that was all."

According to my own mother, ever cynical about romance as associated with anyone in her ex-husband's family, none of the Nelson girls were getting married before their big sister Rose, who must have come with a sizable dowry (although whether or not Albert ever collected is also a matter of dispute). My grandparents were married before he was out of law school and the eldest of their three sons, my father, called Nelson for his mother's family, was born in 1932.

Rose tapped the horn lightly when she picked me up in Pelham to take me to see my father in New Jersey. She was everybody's chauffeur, in a silver, two-door Mercedes XL. This was her pleasure, her job, we assumed, and part of her definition as Grandmother. We roundly abused her, but Rosie was the boss—the original control freak, the ultimate meddler—that was my grandma. In spite of her erect posture and perfect grammar, Grandma never got out of the car to ring the doorbell when she came to pick me up at my mother's house. This was her ex-daughter-in-law, after all, and they had never reconciled. Rose sat with the keys in the ignition and the radio on, tapped the horn two times, lowered the passenger window and cupped her hands to her mouth: "Yoo hoo, yoo hoo, Dinah!" she called if the weather was good and the windows were open and I heard her, whether I was waiting at the front door or up in my room, on the third floor facing the backyard.

Yoo hoo. She sang it to us in shopping malls and restaurants, at the zoo, at the beach, in airports and train stations, from the cash register at the Stop and Shop. When we got to be teenagers we plagued her with it like a Bronx cheer, obnoxious, from the kitchen table to the sink where she was loading the dishwasher while we picked at cold chicken and fruit salad.

"Yoo hoo, Grandma," we cupped our hands to our mouths, "more Hawaiian Punch, if you please, Granny, yoo hoo."

We none of us got up to get it ourselves. She was the designated waitress, after all.

She was food obsessed, Grandma was, food governed her days, and whether this is a fact of nature or nurture, her obsession is our collective inheritance, continues to drive us, generation after generation. All of us eat too fast and directly from cartons, from Tupperware; we stand next to the fridge and gorge on cold fried rice in sticky lumps; we stand in the pantry with one hand deep in an open box of Wheat Thins; we lean over the sink, working on ice cream by the pint, freezer burn not withstanding. We pretend every time it's just a taste we want, just a spoonful or two, "No, no, thanks, no, don't need a bowl, don't need a plate, don't want to sit down."

True, this is cultural, American Jews are obsessed with food, and even bigger than that, the American upper middle classes are obsessed with food, but in our cases, my father's, my uncles', my cousins', and mine, it can all be traced to Rose.

"How much do you weigh?" she was apt to ask, before the car door had slammed behind me, before I'd buckled myself in or had a chance to inhale the smell of leather and pipe smoke that overtook me, deliciously so, the moment I slid into my seat.

"Put the button down, Dinky," she said in singsong. Then, again, as she was pulling out from the curb, again she asked in her perfect singsong, "So, dear, how much do you weigh?"

She, herself, weighed 140 pounds, no matter what she ate, no matter when, no matter how old or young she was, she always weighed 140 pounds. No cookies in her cabinets. No nuts or chips in the pantry, only water-packed tuna and rye crisps in bulk. She rarely allowed my grandfather dessert when they went out to dinner. She tried her best to deny him a shot of bourbon on his eightieth birthday but my father said, "Jesus, Dad, you're eighty, have a bourbon if you want, have two."

Rose was audacious. She showed up late to my wedding in a white sequined dress with matching beret, strutted into the garden announcing her arrival, "Excuse me, excuse me, please, I'm the Grandmother, I'm the *Grandmother*," until she found herself a front-row spot. She was appalled when she saw my dress, moiré with its own subtle bit of sheen, and after the ceremony she practically wagged her finger in my face. "Dinah, you told me you weren't wearing white! I'd never have worn this ensemble!"

And Rose was devoted. My father never saw me perform on stage, was singularly unenthused unless he could watch me on prime time television. Grandma, though, never missed a production, near or far. She made her way to every show I ever did, in remote locales and oddball venues, suited and bejeweled, with Grandpa in tow, decked out in primary colors, outrageous prints (think blue whales on yellow pants) and fantastic bow ties. In New Hampshire, where I played in nonunion summer stock for a couple of years, they stayed in a bed and breakfast not far from an old red barn of a theater, bats in the balcony and field mice in the wings.

Rose, who had never been able to leave a roll in a basket, once entered from the back of the house in the middle of a daytime rehearsal of *Cabaret* calling, "Yoo hoo, yoo hoo, Dinah, I brought muffins!"

The director turned in disbelief, all actors and stagehands rendered speechless, watching my grandmother sashay down the aisle to make her delivery, a package of mushed breakfast pastries wrapped in pink paper napkins which she thrust into the hands of the stage manager, while I stood gaping, frozen to my spot on the stage. She was oblivious to my humiliation, or else she simply didn't care, and even I knew, seething with anger, just how fetching she was. What would be deemed interfering, obnoxious in a parent, was adorable in a grandmother, after all.

Rose and Al visited us in LA once a year and until Eliza was born they stayed with us in the guest room, quaintly furnished, fresh flowers on the night tables, which did not for a moment distract Rose from the fact of our dubious location above downtown Los Angeles and far, far away from the Pacific Ocean.

She had a niece, my second cousin, who still lives on the fashionable West Side, in a house that smacks of Santa Fe, all terra cotta tile and oversized, overstuffed furniture. When I was just a few months pregnant with my first child, Rose arranged for all three of us to have lunch together in Hollywood, which is sort of the halfway point between Cindy's house and mine.

At this juncture it's important to note how much Rose hated the Dodge, the stripper, the car I'd inherited from my father-in-law. She perched on the seat with a rigid spine, ready to jump out at the first opportunity, and she longed out loud for air conditioning. She lowered the window for a bit of a breeze only to lose her curls to a hot wind. She raised it to save her hair and almost immediately started to sweat. It was midsummer in Los Angeles, a ribbon of smog curving brown around the city, and I didn't love the Dodge either, but I was damned if I'd admit it, A, and B, would she rather take a city bus?

We got to the restaurant early and parked a half a block away. Cindy found us at a table a few moments later. She was wearing a spectacular burgundy silk dress with velvet trim at the neck, flowing, expensive, terribly chic. She smelled wonderful.

"Look," she stage-whispered, as though I was her best friend and confidante and not a relative she never saw. "Look what Brian just gave me." Brian was her husband.

She flicked her long streaky hair away from her face with one hand and held the other wrist across the table, fingers dangling gracefully and perfectly manicured in the French style, clear and shiny with white-rimmed tips, to show off her new Rolex—square, chunky, very gold—she preferred it, she explained, to the models for women.

"Oh, Cindy, isn't that beautiful?" said Rose, looking very closely at the watch, then taking all of her in, slim, blond, tastefully accessorized, while I sat on my ever-widening bottom (I was pregnant, remember) and tallied the many ways that I could be made to feel inferior in a matter of moments.

In the seconds between the toss of her mane and the extension of her arm, I'd decided that I hated my clothes, my hair,
my face, my body, too, and I'd put my own hands—peeling
nails, callused thumbs and only a wedding band, no diamonds,
no gems—in my lap to avoid inspection.

Lunch arrived. I was hungry enough to pick up my fork and
eat my way through a trough of Pasta Mama, spaghetti with
scrambled eggs and cheese, without thinking about my un-
sightly fingers. Rose and Cindy picked, and Cindy regaled us
with stories about her glamorous life as the personal assistant
to a movie star.

At the end of the meal, my grandmother took Cindy's
hands in hers. "If anything should happen to me, darling,"
she said, eyes full, "promise me you'll take care of your Uncle
Al."

I watched the two of them, caught in a clinch, fingers inter-
twined, brimming with emotion as if they were everything to
each other.

Outside the restaurant, Cindy embraced my grandmother
one more time. Then she walked around one corner, and
Rose and I took the turn around the other, both of us silent,
Rose rummaging with one hand in her beautiful Gucci bag. I
opened the passenger door for her before I slid into my own
seat and rolled down my window. I put the key in the ignition.
I could contain myself no longer.

"My God, Grandma," I exploded, "*Cindy* should take care
of *Grandpa*? First of all, you'll outlive him by about fifty years
and second of all, he's *my* grandfather—you're staying in *my*
house—you're visiting *me*! If anyone's going to take care of
him, *I* am. Got that?"

Rose sniffed, still fishing for something to wipe her nose.

"Whatever you say, dear," she murmured out the window.

I snorted. I pulled out of my parking space and jerked the
car into second, screeching backwards at the top of the hill,

before I got back into first and turned east onto Fountain Avenue.

"Oh dear," sighed Grandma, dabbing now at her eyes with a crumpled piece of Kleenex from the bottom of her bag. "Dear, dear," she sighed again, stuffing the tissue back inside and rolling down her window a quarter of an inch. "I wish I knew," she said with a cluck of the tongue, with real regret, "I *wish* I knew, don't you, darling, what Cindy drives."

I have an old black and white photograph of Rose and Al, framed on a shelf behind glass in the breakfront in my living room. They're dancing, and she's beautiful in a white dress, off the shoulder, black hair, narrow black eyes practically disappearing in her wide-mouthed smile.

In another photo, also black and white, they sit on the steps of a brick and ivy building, a Cambridge dorm, it must be, wearing matching caps and gowns on the day of my grandfather's graduation from law school. She's one step above him, with her arm draped around his shoulder, proprietary, proud, a little sexy even. Grandma sent me these photos and others—pictures I'd sent her first—of me, of my children. She forgot how she got them and that she ought to be sentimentally attached—she took pinking shears to most of them, cut them into oblongs, trapezoids, weird triangles with scalloped edges. She was averse to your average rectangle, loathe to allow for conventional framing. She butchered those photos in the throes of creative frenzy.

Rose was a painter, and a sculptor, too. I have the bust she did of my grandfather, missing the tip of one ear (a shipping casualty) and the round-framed glasses that used to sit on his nose, who knows where they are? She didn't get much credit for her efforts because Albert was the prize in this marriage, the paragon of intellect and talent straight through his retirement and beyond. She took him, circa 1975, through a welders' gallery, and he told her, "Any idiot can do this." She dared him to try, and he made a second career of it, showing his work, enormous steel obelisks, mobiles and monuments—big as prehistoric birds—in New York galleries and shows. But she was the inspiration and the instigator, and when we were too flip, too condescending, too rude at her expense, he cut us down fast.

"Don't you ever," he said in flat, New England tones, "don't you ever talk to your grandmother that way. Don't you know she's the love of my life?"

Which we would have forgotten because we each of us labored under the delusion that we were the brightest star, the love of his life and hers. That was their gift to us.

"No, no," one of my cousins might interrupt at this point. "No, no, Dinky, *you* were the favorite."

Was this true? If so, only because my father was the eldest and my mother the most beautiful, and I, the sole survivor of that perfect, if doomed union, the singular vessel for all that brilliance. Limited access further enhanced my status, in my own eyes at least. It was always special when they saw me, always treats and holidays and spoiling because it was so rare. Grandpa never failed to put a big bill in my pocket, and Grandma sent me a check for a hundred dollars a month well into my twenties because I was an actress and lived in a sixth floor walk-up on Second Avenue and waited tables deep into the night for a living, and she was desperately worried (can you even believe it?) I might not get enough to eat.

I wasn't around enough to know what I was missing: they'd taken this cousin to England and that one to Russia and that one to Spain; they'd paid for this cousin's tuition and that one's car; they ate dinner with their other grandchildren on a weekly basis; they vacationed with their sons' families every summer at the Jersey shore. I believed my grandparents absolutely when they told me I was the best, the most adored, and

I was enough preoccupied with my own navel that I fancied myself some sort of celebrity guest in their midst, unaware of the toxic cloud—equal parts guilt, pity and regret—wafting over and around me wherever I went.

Grandpa was brilliant and Grandma was a well-appointed tugboat. Sturdy. Steady. Reliable and well-constructed. For as long as any of us could remember, she'd buzzed with stamina, fairly vibrated with energy, dragging him along on this or that excursion and telling him all the while to pick up his feet.

"Don't shuffle, Al," she reprimanded him from over her shoulder, always a pace or so ahead, stopping every so often to make sure she hadn't left him behind.

But one February morning I called to ask how she was. Usually, she'd say, with a giggle, she couldn't believe she was eighty-one (or -two or -three or -four), she felt just as she had at seventeen when she first met Grandpa, it was only her own reflection that reminded her. On this day, though, she complained that her eyes were bothering her. "I don't know what's the matter with me, Dinah. I'm not feeling well at all."

We spoke only briefly because she thought she might go back to bed for a while. The next day she had a massive stroke from which neither she nor my grandfather ever recovered. A week later her sons decided to remove life support, not without argument and tears, and only days afterward we buried her in a Jewish cemetery in Ridgewood, New Jersey, alongside her beloved father and mother. When I took my grandfather's elbow after the ceremony, he seemed tiny to me, frail and stooped, gripping my arm, stumbling from the grave up to the road and back to the car.

I can't remember when Neil was married, how much time elapsed, only that Rose was conspicuously absent, that Albert arrived with Eva, his nurse, and sat between us with his right hand—spotted and wrinkled—held in my lap between my two. No longer interested in social niceties, he managed his way into the pew on his own steam—*don't shuffle, Al*—only to ask, staring hard across the aisle at Iris, Noel's sister, whom he'd met a hundred times, "Who the hell is that?" When I answered, he remarked, full-voiced, "God, she's aged . . ."

The bridesmaids—how many were there?—assembled in the back of the church and began their synchronized walk, the bride in their wake, an endless procession culminating in a semicircle at the altar, May sunshine, stained glass, a robed priest, and a moment of perfect silence.

"Dear God," said my grandfather with great urgency.

"What is it?" I whispered.

"I've no choice at all, none whatsoever, I must relieve my bladder or all will live to regret it."

He was himself but not himself, as eloquent as always, but when we broke up in our pews, silently shaking, felled by the joke like dominoes, Albert never noticed.

When had he started to slip away from us? Only a short time before that wedding, and less than a year after Rose died—still present, albeit grieving—he called me in LA one morning just to chat.

"Dinah," he said, pausing for effect, "I saw your grandmother last night. She came to me, darling—not a dream, not at all—she was there in the room, smiling, beautifully gowned. She waved and left through the French doors on the other side of the bed.

"Her headstone has finally been finished, you know," he added. "Naturally, I cannot help but link the two events."

13 | Acting

I get my call time from *Cracker*. Wednesday midmorning I'm
due to drive up the Golden State Freeway to the flats of Valen-
cia to play a scene with the star; he's the genius detective, and
I'm a psychiatrist to a transsexual killer with baby lust who has
stolen an infant from a hospital nursery. The Monday before, I
go for my fitting with my pager clipped to my jeans. The sizes
I asked for are too big and they have to pull more clothes from
the wardrobe truck. I stare into the mirror at that peculiar
face—almost gaunt—and I have fantasized gaunt for as long as
I can remember. But gaunt or not, I hardly recognize her, that
woman in the mirror whose father is missing.

Tuesday night Paul calls to say the real-life detectives are
getting close, they know where he is, helicopters are hovering
over the New York side of the Hudson, searching in circles, a
loud light show along the Hudson River.

"It's not good, Dine," he says. "It's not good."

I call my stepmother and leave a message on her machine.

Everything is the same gray color at five o'clock Wednesday
morning, when I open my eyes just before the phone rings on
my side of the bed. I pick it up and stumble over to the win-

dow, where the buzz in the line goes away, blocking my left
ear with my index finger to hear better. Fred is beside me, his
hand on my arm.

"Dinah, they found him," says Paul.

"Is he dead?"

"Yes—yes."

He tells me he will call later in the day to tell me about the
memorial service and to get my flight information.

"Paul, can I ask you a favor?"

"You'll say a few words at the service," he answers, but
that's not what I want. I ask him to get me something, anything—a watch, cufflinks—before it's all gone, something that
belonged to my father that I can have for my children.

No reply, something muttered, muffled, a shuffling in the
background, a woman's voice rises in a question.

"Paul? Hello?" I press harder against my left ear with the
heel of my palm.

"Dinah," says Gayle, who has taken the phone, "he's crying,
honey, what did you say to him?"

It's just after seven that morning when I call my manager at
home.

"They found my father," I say. "I can't work today."

"You can't work?"

I woke her, I can tell, she's confused, distracted by her own
small daughter who is whining in the background. In a voice
that's higher and flatter than my own, I explain that my father is dead, found in the woods in a ravine by the Hudson
River. As I speak it's as though I'm on the other side of the
room, watching, listening, wondering who can be saying these
words.

After I hear from Paul and once we've gotten the kids off to
school, I clean up my desk, make phone calls, reservations,
pack an overnight bag. That afternoon, Fred and I retrieve Jake

from the jcc and we drive all together to pick up Eliza from her school, in the flats of West LA. We park, as always, in the lot behind Winston Tires, next to an overflowing dumpster. The sun, a washed out ball in a no-color sky, is September hot in this part of town, all squat and the same, no relief from the scorching, and the hills in all directions have disappeared behind the smog.

We buckle the kids in behind us, then turn around in our seats to talk to them: family conference in the car. Eliza, initially delighted to see us both, grows suddenly suspicious, knows something is up, leans forward in her seat and knits her brows.

"Pop died," I say.

Jake struggles to understand. "So we will never see him again?"

There was an accident involving the car, we explain, and Eliza asks, "Was he wearing a seat belt?"

"Pop never wore his seat belt," says Jake, and then, "Too bad we won't get to see him one more time." He begins to cry, silently.

Eliza, studying her lap, says, "I need privacy to think about this."

"I wish," Jake chokes out, "I wish I was with Pop right now."

Before we start home, we tell them that I must go back East for a few days, to say good-bye.

"I want to say good-bye," says Jake. "I want to come with you to say good-bye to Pop."

My uncle has pressed me to leave the kids home, as if I needed convincing. Back in New Jersey the smallest of the cousins know the details of what happened to their grandfathers' brother, but I'm not ready to tell my own children, and I'm grateful not to have to.

That night, just hours after my father's body has been found, we have tickets to see the Dodgers, and we cannot disappoint these kids. Do I look different, I wonder, sitting in the stands, a week after my father has been kidnapped and murdered, the day his body has been discovered on the banks of the Hudson River. Do I smell funny, I wonder, sitting next to my daughter who eats half of her cotton candy, a handful of popcorn, a bite of a hot dog, and hands the remains each in turn to me.

An acquaintance, a mother from the preschool, catches sight of us and wanders down from her seat to whisper in my ear. "Have they found your father?" she wants to know.

"Yes, this morning," I whisper back. "He's dead. I'm leaving tomorrow."

We both stare out over home plate and she knows not to say any more.

"Will you miss me?" I ask Jake, when I kiss him good-bye the following day.

"Mom," he says, "how can you miss someone when you know they're coming back?"

At the airport, I buy the *New York Times*. There he is on the front page of the metro section. "Youths Accused of Killing New Jersey Millionaire," reads the headline, and there's a photo—not the prison mug shot from 1974, a smiling one this time—later I will get a condolence note that remarks on the twinkle in his eye.

Bludgeoned, says the paper, pistol-whipped, hit with a rock in the back of the head, stabbed multiple times, and his throat, says the article, *may* have been cut.

A large black lady in a navy polyester suit sits beside me at gate 40-something, puts her hand on my shoulder. "You all right, miss? Honey? You all right?"

I nod in her direction, focusing on the lint on her shiny sleeve, willing her to leave, willing her to stay, willing myself to disappear, willing it to be yesterday or the day before yesterday, or the week before last.

"You know that man?" she asks, pointing with one dimpled finger, and now the self-conscious dilemma begins, for I am the actress, the eldest, the only child from the first marriage, the one who talked too much, the one who needed too much attention. But if I deny who he is, isn't that wrong? Mustn't I shout this to the terminal? Mustn't I call attention to this evil? Mustn't I stand up and tell everybody, *This is my father*!

She calls to the stewardess who's involved in preflight procedures near the security doors, "Look here, miss, this is awful, this is her *daddy*! Give me this a minute," she says, taking the paper from me. "Look at this here." She's jabbing the photo with her index finger. "This is her *father* in this picture here."

Somehow I rise. "Please," I say, "please, I'm sorry," and I take the newspaper and walk in the direction of the pay phones to call Fred, to tell him, when I can breathe again, the *New York Times* says maybe they cut his throat.

"Oh no," says my husband. "Can you sit down, do you need water, oh, Dine, what can I do?"

Fred has always regretted that he didn't come with me. With his own parents dead, he saw this loss as an inevitable—if extraordinary—rite of passage, one through which he'd always intended to hold my arm, support me, stand at my side.

When Rose died of natural causes, neither of us thought twice about Fred's staying in LA with Eliza and Jake. No point in dragging everybody east for three days, and who else to march the kids through soccer and T-ball and the weekend birthday party parade? I was relieved to learn Leah and Ron would actually be in town for business reasons. Fortuitous, that, especially with Fred suddenly knocked flat by a terrible cold. But when I suggested they coordinate with him and the kids, my mother's fury was unmistakable. As was her contempt for my grandmother, her ex-mother-in-law.

"Dinah," she spat over the wires, "don't expect me to grieve for that woman! She betrayed me!"

Nobody was asking her to grieve, I protested, only to spell Fred for a bit, to take the kids for ice cream, to play a couple of rounds of gin rummy with one or the other and give the poor man a break. My mother was damned, she announced, if she'd facilitate my mourning.

"Don't presume, Dinah," she admonished, opting not to see her own grandchildren that weekend rather than to pick up the slack.

This time, in the wake of my father's murder, Fred felt truly conflicted about letting me fly east alone. Who could blame him under the circumstances? But who else to stay with our children, who only knew their grandfather was dead, and not the truth about how he died? Who better to hold them, and love them, and protect them from the dark?

14 | Eulogies

I used to like to tease my father about keeping in touch.

"You never write, you never call," I taunted him once.

"No news is good news," he countered. "Out of sight, out of mind," he added with a wink.

"No, Dad," I said, stroking the top of his head where his hair was thinning. "Absence makes the heart grow fonder . . ."

Weeks after the service, back home and alone with Fred when the kids are at school or after they're asleep, I'll talk to myself, I'll wonder out loud, I'll voice my confusion and my disbelief. I'll defend my indignation and my sorrow; I'll remind my husband—as if he didn't know—that I used to call my father every couple of weeks. I dutifully thought of him from time to time. Often! I thought about him often! But now, I assert (am I complaining?), I'll think about my father every day, he'll always be with me, *every single day* for the rest of my life! *Does that seem fair to you?* I'll ask Fred.

He won't remind me that his mother wasted away with cancer, was destroyed by the enemy from the inside out, or that his father dropped dead exactly one week after he'd moved to

Southern California to be closer to us. Fred won't pull rank. He'll only say, "I know. Oh Dinah, I'm sorry. I know."

When I close my eyes, I see my father nodding, laughing at the joke. I shake it off and close my eyes again: of course it's fair, it's necessary, expected, mandatory in fact; he's not laughing at all, he's solemn, even grim, as if to emphasize that this is my job and his due, to acknowledge him on a daily basis; that's the only afterlife of which we can be absolutely certain.

"I'm lucky," I will tell the crowd at my father's memorial service. "I have a piece of my father in my little girl with the big heart who needs privacy, and in my little boy with the big heart who looks just like him."

My mother and my sister come to the funeral. The memorial service, that is, which takes place in a Jewish funeral home in northern New Jersey.

"But he wasn't religious," argued my stepmother when she learned where Paul had arranged for the service. "He didn't believe in God," she asserted, she being one of the all-time great self-hating Jews, a Guggenheim on her mother's side, middle-named Noel because she was born on Christmas, and embracing of all things Episcopalian. (When I pierced my ears at age twelve, she complained I looked like an immigrant.)

"He came into this world a Jew and he's going out a Jew," said my Uncle Paul, and that was that.

Gayle points me toward the chapel almost as soon as we arrive. There's a coffin, but it's hard to believe he's inside. What's left of him anyway? I enter before the service and sit alone in the first row, in front of the long box, which is covered with an American flag, because, his brothers decided, he was a patriot, a public servant, and that moves me.

I talk to the man. "Dad," I say. "Dad, are you there?"

Not in the box, right? Surely not in the box. . . . Maybe in the oddly displaced chunk of sunshine on the floor in the corner, seemingly disconnected from the window above, but then I have never been much for light or shadow or the precepts of physics.

"Daddy, come back to me, tell me what happened, tell me you're okay, tell me it doesn't hurt."

Later a friend will lend me *The Tibetan Book of Living and Dying*, and I will learn that it does hurt and that my father's soul is in a constant state of outrage. Later still I will learn from a rabbi that it's over, my father is dust, dead and gone and cannot hear me. Not so long after that a different rabbi will insist that my father lives on, will urge me to pay attention to my dreams where he will visit me. Much, much later I will learn to talk to my father about other things, things having nothing to do with the way he died. For now, though, I have taken Valium for the first time in my life, and I feel wired and strangely calm—out of my body—like a dead person, I think, except I have pins and needles in my fingers as though I'd been sitting on my hands. I leave the coffin and the sanctuary, and my mother hugs me and tells me I look pretty good under the circumstances, and my sister, so poised and lovely, makes me feel proud and bolstered somehow, and my Aunt Gayle points to the receiving line.

"Go," she says.

"I don't know if I should." I am looking to where my stepmother stands beside her son, greeting people as they enter through the heavy double doors.

"Go, Dinah," she presses. "He was your father."

So I go and I meet and greet, like at weddings and Bar Mitzvahs—but this is my father's funeral and my father was murdered. Valium, I realize, is a miracle. A really wonderful drug.

The presiding rabbi here in Hackensack, New Jersey, who also buried my grandmother, takes us all aside just before the service and tells us, sternly, he will not tolerate hysteria. He's worried about the sensational nature of this event, reporters in the chapel and outside, who've been waiting all week for quotes and photo opportunities.

"We are here to remember Nelson," he reminds us, "and to mourn him. If I think things are getting out of hand I'm going to stop this thing."

First a new friend, a golf buddy, Alfred Taubman, who's since been jailed for fixing prices in a scandal involving Sotheby's Auction House, comes to the pulpit on the raised platform in front of the stained glass. He's been asked to eulogize a man he knew just well enough to invite to Scotland on his private plane. Having learned a whole lot from the newspapers over the last week, his eulogy is well-intentioned but oddly biographical, like a regurgitated obituary from the *Bergen Record* but only the good stuff. It's vaguely apologetic, this tribute to my father: *I'm sorry I didn't know this guy too well, I'm sorry this awful thing has happened, I'll pretend we were better friends than we were for your sakes, and because I am the most important person in the room.*

Next a woman addresses the congregation (a neighbor from the Hamptons?), someone I've never met, blond, diminutive, and smart. Her words are strong, heartfelt, and I know she really knew the man and cared for him, which is a relief to me after the first speaker, and I'm thankful.

Then my turn, I begin on a sob. Later my mother will say she worried I wouldn't be able to keep it together, and my sister will tell me that as I stepped up to the microphone, a woman in front of her whispered, "Oh no, that must be the daughter," but the Valium lingers on, and I'm able to introduce myself to some three hundred mourners.

"I'm Dinah," I say, and they recognize me, I'm certain, as the one who looks like him, the child from the first, brief marriage, most importantly, the mother of the grandchildren he adored.

I wrote my eulogy the night before, in a guest bedroom at my uncle's house.

"You have to speak," Paul had urged on the phone, even before I arrived, exhausted and a little hysterical, having wandered from the baggage claim to the gate over and over because Gayle and I had somehow missed each other. She found me, finally, weeping, struggling with change at a pay phone near the escalators.

Paul, wearing navy blue silk pajamas, watching the news from an easy chair in his bedroom, seems smaller than I remembered when he stands to hug me and says again, "You'll speak, Dinah." He collapses back into his seat.

"No. No. I can't."

"You must. You're the actress," he says, and though I bristle at the idea that I could act my way through an ordeal like this, I'm somehow relieved to be asked.

"I need you to do this," he entreats. "You know I can't."

Paul was the middle child, fortunate to have been neglected in favor of his big brother, my father, the star of the family, destined for greatness; and Michael, the baby, the profligate, the troublemaker, who demanded attention in conventionally negative ways. Quiet Paul—humble, unassuming, loyal and good to his mother—had gone on to marry his high school sweetheart, Gayle, and make a fortune in the insurance business. Even so, as far as I could tell, he had always been fundamentally sheepish and shy.

He runs through tomorrow's program for me, explains that Michael intends to wrap it all up with a speech of his own, and we both roll our eyes, complicit in the knowledge that my father and Michael didn't like each other much. Taubman, the real estate mogul, will go first, he says, but nice a fellow as he is, Paul thinks he can't have much to say about a man he's just recently met on the golf course.

Paul takes a legal pad and a pen from the top of his night table and pushes them into my hands.

"Go on," he orders. "Go write something now. Go write a few words."

Paul is gray now, as Nelson was, but with more hair and heavier, a little doughy in comparison—a cheerful version—as close as I will come, I think, to finding my father. He's all I have left and I want him to love me. I leave the master bedroom with the paper and pen.

The guest room is off a small flight of stairs in the top corner of the rambling, old house. It's like a cabin in a ship, crowded with furniture, dark, with small, irregular windows. I open my bag onto one of the twin beds, hang my suit from the closet door, the funeral suit (I'd worn it the year before when I eulogized my grandmother), bottle-green, designer-labeled, a present from my mother for my thirty-fifth birthday.

How can I possibly be here, alone and all grown up, in my father's brother's house? It's not that I'm uncomfortable with my aunt and uncle. Gayle was good to me when I was small, took me off Nelson's hands in the middle of those longer visits, forged a relationship with me in spite of her own strained communication with my father and Noel, whom she thought were snooty and pretentious. I grew especially close to my cousin Lauren, their daughter, who put me up when I came east to bury Rose. How peculiar that time to meet my father at the funeral home. He'd called a few days before to tell me his mother had "passed away." His voice broke as he said the words and he got off the phone as fast as he could. *Passed away*. An intolerable euphemism, gives me the creeps every time, benign as it is. And so strange, coming from my father, who was neither a believer, nor one for making nice. I'd never use that phrase, not about anyone, and certainly not about him. But even to say *he died*, in my father's case, rings false; he didn't just die, he was killed, which is something entirely different.

My father had called, anyway, to summon me home for my grandmother's funeral, as if anything would have kept me away. No question, though, of my staying with him in Saddle River. I could have, I supposed, but it never even came up; he assumed I'd be with my mother in New York and was mildly surprised, even pleased, to learn moments before the service that I'd spent the night with his brother's daughter, that the trip east hadn't been an excuse for me to visit my other family.

And is he pleased with me now? I wonder. Does he know I'm here in his brother's house? That I've come too late to see him one last time? Too late to say good-bye? It's only when I finally begin—with a list of adjectives scrawled across the paper (inscrutable, powerful, fierce, handsome, tough, explosive, silent, impervious, compassionate, generous, gentle, loyal, tenacious, proprietary, teasing, uncompromising, on and on and on)—that I realize I was right to come alone. Fred, if he were with me, would prop me up, stay close, baby me, and let me wipe my eyes on his shirt sleeve if that was what I wanted to do. But I need this solitary time, to sort my thoughts, to stand tall and strong, to be Nelson's daughter for a few hours, rather than somebody's mother or wife.

My whole self sags, but when sleep finally comes it's like I'm wide awake, except I know I'm alone and have to be dreaming this crowded room, buzzing with people and activity. My husband, my children, drift in and out, call to me, reach past me for something to one side or the other, float away again as if they are traveling on a slow-moving river just beside the bed. Still I'm certain I haven't closed my eyes, except that my grandmother is dead, so I must be dreaming her pacing before me, rearranging my clothes, scrutinizing my belongings, offering me cold chicken, a piece of old melon, wrinkled and tough near the rind, mushy at the top. *I buy fruit, no one eats it,* she says, gliding legless forward and back, dressed just as my grandfather described her in his own night vision.

But in *my* dream she speaks. *I buy fruit, no one eats it.* She doesn't question why we're here together in this attic room. She seems not to know it's the night before her eldest's funeral, or if she does, she's already dead, impervious, indifferent to the shock. Does she know something I don't? Can it be she doesn't care? Either way she's incapable of grieving.

The next morning when I face myself in the lighted mirrors in my aunt's bathroom, I collapse onto a stool, clutching my ribs, unable to breathe, knowing I can't possibly attend this funeral much less speak out loud in front of strangers. The power of this thing—the shock of it—comes on again like a giant wave, takes me under, thrashes me about, leaves me wasted, bedraggled until next time. I only know its strength in these violent episodes, and then I'm just me again, just an ordinary person on the beach, panting hard, waiting to be caught in riptide, swallowed up and spat out. Gayle comes into the bathroom with her blow dryer, to find me doubled over and gasping, scolds me for being weak, administers drugs, the excellent Valium, enables me to carry on.

"My father should have lived to see my kids grow up," I will say near the end of my speech. I know the mourners are studying my face—taking in my hair, dark, my features, strong, my height, considerable, my eyes, slanting like his.

Afterward a friend named Geoffrey, young and handsome and rich, married to an equally smooth blonde, neither of whom I have ever met before, will follow me around the property, corner me when he can, to talk about my father and justice and keeping his memory alive. Boldly he'll look me up and down, search my face, stare without embarrassment or apology. He'll tell me he can't get over his first glimpse of me, earlier that day, when I stood up for my father. "It was like Nelson was standing there," he will say again and again. Week after week he will call me from the East Coast to talk about the crime, about vengeance, until my husband grows uneasy and I grow less voluble and the calls finally get scarce and peter out.

"My father should have lived to be a hundred," I will say from the pulpit. "I don't want to imagine him hurt. I don't want to imagine him weak. I cannot imagine him old. I cannot imagine him gone."

15 | Christmas with Dogs

"It's not her fault, she can't help it, it's that mother of hers," Rose would say in defense of her daughter-in-law when she was rude or dismissive with one or the other of us.

Sometime in the early '90s, Noel, brown-eyed, got herself an assortment of colored contact lenses. Ever ingratiating I complimented her, straight-faced, when I first saw the blue ones.

"Well, they're so natural on me," she agreed, and as evidence of their authenticity she pointed to her mother's failure to notice the difference when she wore them.

"But Noel," Audrey had remarked, when confronted with the truth of the colored lenses, "haven't your eyes always been blue?"

All that wealth and privilege, but her own mother didn't know the color of her eyes.

Once when she was especially mean, I asked Ron why he thought my father allowed her to mistreat me.

"It's simple, Dinah," my stepfather explained. "He has to live with *her*."

When Noel and I made a stab or two at staying in touch

after the murder, my mother was incredulous. "At least with him dead," she groaned, "at the very least, you two shouldn't have to deal with each other any more."

By the middle of December, 1984, Fred, whom I'd met toward the end of the summer, had pretty much moved in. He kept two suits in my closet and they were both awful. His first wife married him in spite of the brown, which I'd managed to shove all the way to the back behind some dry cleaning wrapped in plastic, just in case polyester turned out to be contagious. I wondered every time I saw him in it, how his mother, who died long before I met him, could have let her only son walk down the aisle in that jacket. He couldn't have grown since then, so the sleeves must always have hung, as they did now, to just above his wrist bones. As for the black number, newer, with narrower lapels and not quite so spongy, it was innocuous but it made him look like a maitre d'.

For this, our first Christmas, I shopped at Brooks Brothers and came home with an argyle sweater vest, a pin-striped button-down shirt, and a paisley tie that brought together the whole ensemble. I didn't know yet (I wouldn't catch on for years), that my future husband had a profound aversion to all things preppy, so my pleasure was uncompromised when I saw him all dressed up. Fred, mostly considerate if not unfailingly polite, was not about to let me know at this point in our relationship that I'd gotten him wrong. He'd been advised it would be a difficult day regardless of what he wore, besides which he was in love.

We'd been invited, my new boyfriend and I, to Christmas dinner with my father and his family. I'd never spent the holiday anywhere else—Christmas with Nelson was a clause in the contract—and in all those years I'd never invited a friend. I'd never been given the option, for one thing, and for another, most friends had their own Christmas obligations; even if they didn't, I'd have been afraid to ask anyone to accompany me before now.

Years ago, in high school, I'd brought my friend Anna along one summer weekend. Since my stepmother is fluent in Italian, I thought she'd be impressed; Anna's parents had emigrated from Rome when she was a baby and the family spoke Italian at home. Anna was beautiful, petite with full breasts and full lips, olive skin and a mane of black hair that she wrapped around her head at night to straighten. She wore faded bell-bottoms over black Danskin leotards and shared her Marlboros with her mother, although we agreed she would refrain in front of my father and his wife. Turned out, Noel wasn't interested in speaking Italian to Anna. She gave us a tour of the house, told us exactly how much the oversized chandelier had cost when she bought it with her Roman-born decorator, and then shooed us, in English, to change down at the pool house so we wouldn't make a mess in the guest bath.

I'll confide, too, that later the same summer over another long weekend I carelessly left a letter from Anna in the bedroom I shared with Aida, Noel's housekeeper. Her tiny room was across the hall from Neil's and directly above the guest suite at the bottom of a narrow flight of stairs. How was it I roomed with Aida—no consideration for her privacy or preference—who went to bed with her face slathered in cold cream and her hair under a kerchief? I never questioned the arrangement. For one thing, I didn't want to share with Neil, eight years my junior, to whom I never felt remotely related or attuned. Happily, the guest room, cold, dark, finely appointed and covered in plastic, wasn't an option. Aida's presence was comforting to me, as was the drone of the black and white set in one corner of her darkened room. As for Anna's letter, discovered under the night table, it confided in some detail about sex with her boyfriend, a high school senior. I think she used the word "balling" and—who could blame them?—my father and Noel were alarmed enough to contact my mother to ask if she was aware of the class of people I was meeting in my ninth grade year. What kind of a community was Pelham anyway? How many of my friends were Italian anyway? Why hadn't I learned to play golf, come to think of it? Or bridge?

I hadn't brought a friend to the house since that time, although I'd been tempted to invite one of my college roommates, who'd grown up in Main Line Philadelphia and prepped at St. Paul's, and whom my stepmother had met in New Haven and pronounced to be very *attractive*. Not long after I started college, though, my father was indicted and convicted of campaign fraud in a New Jersey gubernatorial election and sent to serve prison time at Allenwood. From then on, even after his release, I hardly ever went to Saddle River anymore, and when I did nobody seemed much up to the idea of company. It was enough for my father to visit me at school and treat me and a friend to lunch at Mory's where we ate tomato aspic and Welsh rarebit and then fell asleep afterwards in Psychology 101, woozy from all that butter and an illegal cocktail or two.

Anyway. I'd warned Fred about what to expect—this wouldn't be a warm, fuzzy holiday—it would be tense and uncomfortable because these people, as far as I could tell, weren't warm and fuzzy with each other, never mind me. It didn't occur to me back then that I brought out the worst in them, even knowing I was the thorn in my stepmother's side. Nobody could have convinced me Nelson and Noel were capable of mutual enjoyment whether I was around or not. My father and his wife spoke to each other with what sounded to me like boredom and irritation, if not disrespect. But who was I to judge? They were married for nearly forty years; I've been married long enough now myself to understand that husbands and wives aren't always polite to each other, precisely because they don't have to be. Then, too, Christmas must have been especially fraught for Noel. On top of having to share her birthday with most of the Western world, never once in her long-married life—not until after I moved to California—was the unfortunate woman permitted to celebrate without her husband's daughter in tow.

But that particular Christmas. Christmas, 1984. Fred was thrilled to come along. His mother was dead and his father didn't celebrate until after Boxing Day in order to take best advantage of the store-wide sales. His sister lived outside Boston with her husband and a new baby and he only wanted to be with me. For Fred, orphaned though he was that particular December, Christmas was easy, natural, inevitable to boot. He'd grown up with all the trimmings and he still looked forward to the day like a kid.

For me, Christmas was complicated. First off, it was just one more thing that made me *different*. I'd worked so hard to be absorbed into a family, to be fully integrated as the eldest child and sibling of four. But that family didn't celebrate Christmas. My mother and Ron were culturally observant Jews, even if they didn't believe in God. They didn't do Christmas or any of its trappings, even and especially after we moved to Pelham, a parochial town just north of New York City, where I was one of three Jews in my graduating class in high school. Different again: tall, dark, be-spectacled, and heavy into orthodontics; okay, it's a rare adolescent who feels comfortable in her pimply skin, but did I have to be *Jewish* too?

I looked for an up side: The fact that I was Christmas savvy might have won me some points at Pelham High, where being Jewish was so weird, except I still lived most of the time with those obstinate parents of mine who righteously refused to surrender to a nice, pagan tree and a few measly lights across the widow's walk.

Every Christmas until I could drive, Rose picked me up and

took me over the George Washington Bridge to my father's house in Saddle River. It was a forty-minute trip to the Jersey side of the Hudson but it might as well have been another country. My other family, the Lenneys, went off to places like Florida or North Carolina or Washington DC, in pursuit of warmer climes or cultural enrichment, while I joined my father, his wife, and their son for skiing in Vermont or Colorado at best; at worst, for long, silent days during which I felt entirely unwelcome and wondered why I had to be there at all since nobody seemed to care one way or another, except that it was part of a binding agreement.

Whatever the time of year, winter or summer, I made furtive calls home from that quasi-guest room off the back stairway. I was afraid to admit I was homesick, and I didn't want to be caught wanting my mother, much-hated outwardly by my stepmother, more deeply and dangerously, I suppose, by my father, who wouldn't so much as speak her name. I closed the door behind me and whispered to her from the arm of the cling-wrapped gold-brocade-upholstered sofa. (My mother wondered at all that plastic when I described it. That sort of thing, she explained to me, came with new money and didn't mesh with Noel's upper crust background at all.) Afterward I raided the kitchen for chips and dip and crackers and candy and soda—foods we didn't keep in the pantry at home—then looked for laxatives in the medicine chest or, when I got a little older, stuck my fingers down my throat. My father pushed me off on my grandparents and my cousins for a day here, an overnight there. Once or twice he took me to a roller rink where he sat in the bleachers and read the sports pages while I went round and round on my rented skates, pausing every now and then to mash my nose and lips up against the glass between us to make him laugh.

There were other special events, of course: bowling, for instance, and the circus (where he actually let me see the freak show in its own special tent); he bought me hot chestnuts in Manhattan and penny candy in Quogue and when I ordered steak for dinner in a restaurant he didn't so much as blink. ("Why is it that your daughter always has to have the most expensive thing on the menu?" Noel would murmur just loud enough for me to hear. "Why don't you shut up?" he'd say into his drink. Even if I was secretly pleased to hear him say it, they frightened me when they spoke to each other that way. At *home*, the grown ups never said "shut up" and it was grounds for punishment if one of us did.)

Often a baby-sitter, the niece of one of my father's business partners who was just a few years older than I, took me on field trips to the movies, to theme parks, to Bloomingdale's or Sam Goody. And I played with the girl who lived across the street when she was home from boarding school. We ate Wonder Bread toast slathered with margarine, and rode one of her ponies, and sneaked into her older brother's apartment in the guesthouse where he kept stacks of old *Playboys* under his unmade bed. Alone I chewed on onion grass and picked blackberries and crab apples and acted out adventures that involved the woods and the brook and three old chicken coops, perfect hideouts, empty, cool, and dark in the summer. Whatever the season, I counted the days until I could return home, where reentry was difficult nonetheless, where I felt compelled, back at school after those winter vacations, to casually mention the skiing at Vail, the swimming pool frozen solid in the backyard, the tennis courts, the jukebox in the ballroom and all the presents I'd gotten for *Christmas*.

It would take me a good thirty-six hours to settle back into my real life. I would sulk and shuffle my feet until I'd reestablished my rhythms; empty the dishwasher, set the table, roll the socks, fold the napkins, strum the guitar, disappear into a book, or just flop down across my own bed in my own room and stare into space and, what a relief, ultimately, to be where

I belonged, as much as I belonged anywhere and however odd I was for having disappeared during a family vacation.

Back then divorce wasn't so common, and I was considered a child of a "broken home" which galled me somehow. My home wasn't broken, my home was just fine when I was in it, when I wasn't distracted by this extraneous relationship entirely unique to me. I missed my father, but it was easy to forget in my mother's house, to pretend—along with my mother and Ron—that he didn't exist. Certainly I didn't want to be caught talking about him, calling him *Dad* in my stepfather's presence. This smacked of disloyalty, I thought, and I believed in my core that those sorts of references, those reminders of my true lineage, pegged me for a fraud, an impostor, in this *real* family.

But I've wandered away again from Christmas, 1984, when I was all grown up and able to drive my new boyfriend, Fred, over the George Washington Bridge and into New Jersey all by myself. We went west on Route 4 and north on 17 where I worried over which exit to take, in spite of having traveled this route a hundred times.

We pulled into the gravel lot behind the renovated barn, part garage, part ballroom, French doors on all sides and stored furniture under white sheets. Pressing our faces to the glass on our way to the house, I showed Fred this enormous room where I'd danced by myself as a kid, played movie star, lain flat on my sunburned back against cool, marble floors. This was the room where the buffet would be after my father's memorial service, the only social occasion I would remember ever attending in my father's home, where I was always a stranger, where, if they entertained, I was never around to spy from the fringes as children do. I supposed there were parties—ice-clinking, fox-trotting, air-kissing, eating-and-drinking gatherings there—only not when I was around. Christmas being the exception, of course.

"Be here at three," my father had commanded the week before. When I reminded him that Noel had asked us to come after four, he'd said firmly, "Three," and then, unusually expansive, "We'll want you at three, no later." Something about cocktails, hors d'oeuvres, conversation. Conversation? With my father? He was loving this, playing the grand host before we'd even arrived, and his jocularity was contagious.

We walked the slate path to the house, no snow, but the grass was frozen and gray with winter, and I felt the cold pressing against my ears, between my legs, along my fingers wedged deep in the pockets of my coat. Fred hooked his arm through mine, properly impressed with the wide brick stairs leading down to the pool, empty of water but strewn with leaves and needles from the trees scattered across the property. Beyond the pool, beyond the slope dotted with fruit trees, I pointed to where the tennis courts were hidden behind a row of tall pines. On the front stoop, Fred stood behind me as I knocked (because this was not my house and I never just walked in) before I tried the knob and opened the door. Only Barclay and Darwin, two perfectly coiffed, silver standard poodles, were there to greet us. They sniffed for a moment, then, uninterested, settled themselves in front of the fire on the other side of the hall.

"Hello," I called from the foyer, adjacent to the living room, all walls and an entire floor of the eighteenth-century structure having been blasted away to make for a high-ceilinged great room with enormous wood beams. Stiff high-backed chairs clustered around gilded tables and across from oddly lumpy sofas, museum furniture, it looked to be, carefully arranged on enormous, pale, oriental rugs. The walls were covered in fabric and a gold-framed mirror the size of a small bedroom stood high enough over the fireplace to reflect the dining room on the balcony above. It was formal, this room, palatial, even; it should probably have been cordoned off with ropes of red velvet. Even the dogs, staring into the flames, ought not to be touched.

"Hello?" I ventured, beckoning Fred to follow me further into the room.

"Dad? We're here!"

Nothing. Aida wasn't in the kitchen, up six or seven stairs and off the landing, where I'd tiptoed, leaving Fred uncertain of himself just inside the front door. To reassure him, to protect him, I kept him in my periphery as I peered into the room, long and narrow like a ship's galley, wood-paneled, smelling of sautéed mushrooms and garlic, with small bowls of minced parsley and scallions on the stainless counter by the sink and something simmering in a double boiler on the stove.

I tiptoed back down to Fred—a bit of a feat in high-heeled patent leather pumps—guilty, nervous, a trespasser in my father's house.

"Dad?" I tried again from the front hall, throwing my voice to the master suite, where, now that I thought about it, I heard the shower running.

Noel's voice, a shriek, exploded from the bedroom. I'd heard it before, but here with my boyfriend beside me it was like the first time, watching him start at its pitch and tone.

"Nelson! *Nel*-son! For God's sake, Nelson, your daughter's here! My God, Nelson, it's only three o'clock!"

Did she think we couldn't hear? Hardly breathing, I looked at Fred who was, thankfully, amused, not afraid of her like me. This is your stepmother? his eyebrows asked. The debutante, the equestrienne, the heiress to the Guggenheim fortune if her mother doesn't leave it all to the Metropolitan Museum of Art? That's who this is?

I skittered over to him in my fancy footwear, grabbed his arm and pulled him out the door, careening across the frozen lawn like an amateur burglar. Lucky for me, because I never looked, no one was coming the other way when I tore out the drive on to Chestnut Ridge Road, back to Route 17 to Route 4 to the Binghamton in Edgewater, my father's restaurant, the monster ferryboat moored on the Hudson River that served three hundred covers on a decent night. Now here came a role that I'd only tried on every once in a while: drinks, hors d'oeuvres, conversation, I was determined to have them, to save face, I guess. I twirled on my barstool with exaggerated flair as though I knew how to be the owner's daughter. With feigned confidence I ordered us a bottle of Moet and a dozen oysters, and I charged it all to Dad.

By a quarter to five we found our way back to the house. My father greeted us as though nothing out of the ordinary had occurred. I mumbled an apology to Noel, who smiled at something just over my shoulder and asked if we liked the tree. Fred was introduced all round: to my father, to Noel, to Iris, her sister, a renowned archeologist who wore the family kilts with a crested dagger in her sock; to Iris's friend, Zoe, a famous columnist, with a golden bob and a southwestern twang; to Audrey, Noel's mother, whose hair shone shoe-polish black and whose skin stretched like an old flesh-colored bathing cap across her narrow skull. She was in her nineties, with toothpick arms, and she trembled when she spoke, beautifully, with a mid-Atlantic lilt. Her escort, whose name I've forgotten, was a man in his sixties, slim, coiffed, and affable, like something out of a Noel Coward play.

I distributed my tasteful presents, books, CDs, Godiva chocolates, and orchids in Italian clay pots. Audrey, mortified to receive a gift from me, scurried as best she could on legs like dry kindling to rustle up something from Noel's closet and came back with a box of chocolate-covered cherries wrapped in paper that had been crumpled and smoothed flat again. My half-brother Neil handed me a bottle of Soave Bolla with the yellow price sticker under the red ribbon tied around the neck. Fred, seated beside my father on the sofa, was just eating this up. A drink in one hand, a canapé in the other, he brimmed with amusement and good cheer, as comfortable and game as I was unsettled and awkward.

Iris and Zoe, as always, had brought their dogs, two ancient dachshunds who aimlessly scratched and shimmied over the wood floors. As we paraded to the dining room, one of them, hopelessly drugged for some nervous complaint, slid across the landing like an old woman on skates, through the railings and down, just a foot or so, crashing into a silver coffee tray placed just so on top of the Chinese breakfront below. Much tumult ensued: Iris and Zoe soothed the traumatized dogs while Noel wailed over a dented sugar bowl and my father erupted in his chair, sharing the joke with my happy boyfriend.

Iris got a call from "the countess" in the middle of dinner—roast beef it must have been (when I was thirteen, an impressionable age, Aida roasted baby pigs, snout-to-snout on a platter with crab apples in their mouths, and I swear I have never recovered), candied yams with marshmallow as always, and Brussels sprouts—all served from ornate silver trays by Aida herself, in a white uniform, white stockings, and shoes. Later she would eat her own dinner alone in the kitchen. I had never been permitted to help her clear the table, and my trying, suck-up that I was, didn't win me any points over the years as far as I could tell.

The countess had phoned to wish Iris a merry Christmas, and Zoe for some reason, was none too thrilled with the transcontinental good will. "That bitch," she drawled from her seat on my father's left, and she shouted to Iris, on the extension in the kitchen, that it was rude to take a call in the middle of Noel's birthday dinner. My father, silently quaking in his chair, wiped tears from the corners of his eyes and shared a look with Fred, who was completely entertained. He winked at me, and something about his obvious pleasure allowed me to lean back in my own stiffly upholstered chair and for the first time ever not wonder when it would be time to go home.

For dessert, birthday cake, of course; a many-layered thing with white and dark chocolate shavings on top, which Noel sampled with genuine delight, even before she blew out her candles, as if she hadn't ordered it herself, as if the whole event was a marvelous surprise.

It was here, in Saddle River, that these sisters, Noel and Iris, taught me to put a ring around one of the candles before blowing to make the wish come true. This was a ritual from their girlhood, from boarding school, I suppose. The thing is, I've never been clear about whose wish is in the running; it stands to reason that the birthday person's wish is on the fast track anyway, so we ring bearers must be meant to wish for ourselves. Or are we supposed to push the birthday wish along just in case it gets distracted en route?

Whoever is wishing, I always lend my ring at birthday gatherings, never without thinking of my stepmother, who will be with me for the rest of my life whether we communicate or we don't, because she was my father's wife, because I can't remember a time when she wasn't around, because she's been in my peripheral vision since I was barely a toddler, when logically speaking, I had no peripheral vision at all.

Several years after my father's death, an envelope arrives in February as always, checks enclosed for each of my children, whose birthdays fall within two weeks of each other.

"How do we know Noel again?" Jake asks, contemplating his thank-you note for $150, which he describes in his letter as "more money than I have ever seen."

"Noel was married to Pop," says Fred.

"Have I met her?" Jake asks.

"You have," Fred answers, and Jake signs his letter, *Sincerely, Jake Mills*, which is not so odd when you consider that he has recently conquered cursive and writes out his full name whenever possible.

But who is Noel, to me, to my kids? Is she *family*? Do we get to choose who is family, or do we just belong to each other by virtue of bloodlines, proximity, and shared history? I cringe to think of it, but only Noel and I can possibly remember the week she called me "Kendall" (because she preferred my middle name) and I tried "Mommy," as if we were playing an elaborate game of pretend. She straight-armed me on the day of my father's memorial, so that we wouldn't have to touch, but she sought my gaze on the day of the sentencing, when one of his killers droned his remorse while his own mother rocked in her chair and moaned aloud on the other side of the courtroom. Recently I called Noel about a legal problem having to do with money.

"We all have our troubles," she confided. "My mother is ninety-nine years old, for God's sake, I mean she's living on bread and jam, and she won't part with a penny, let me tell you."

We laughed together and I felt, can I admit it? I felt affection for her, and empathy, too.

"The children, Dinah, that photo you sent. I can't believe it. If you're ever in the neighborhood, I hope you'll bring them to see me," she said.

Noel will always be my stepmother. If I never see her again, and I probably won't, she will retain that label, that relationship to me, specific and undiluted.

But that first Christmas with Fred, with my father, with dogs, there was a twist, a plot turn that I hadn't anticipated or considered. After years of dog day Christmas—clumsy gifts, the wrong clothes, the sense that I didn't belong and shouldn't have come—it never occurred to me that my boyfriend would have a wonderful time. When I asked Fred about that day, he said my father was cordial, good-humored, no-nonsense, and funny. Sure he could be brusque and arrogant, but Fred liked him from that very first meeting.

I never expected anyone to *like* my father, because I'd been raised to hold him in contempt. Each time my husband repeated over the years, to me, to others, that my father was a great guy, I was surprised—unaccountably pleased with them both—happy, but confused. Affection for my father was misguided according to my experience, if not downright traitorous.

16 | Looking for Crumbs

"Did you see him?" asks a friend who cannot help herself, when I call from the airport after the memorial service, on my way back to Los Angeles. "Did you see the body?"

"They wouldn't let us," I say, and I forgive her because I'm also wondering what was left under the yellow tarp.

They wouldn't let us see him, they wouldn't let us see the autopsy report. My stepmother has told me just that afternoon—the two of us standing side by side at the buffet smack in front of a decimated platter of jumbo shrimp and a glass bowl smeared inside and out with what must have been cocktail sauce—that the coroner had assured her she didn't want to see him.

"It was a week," she explained in a canned sort of voice, and I knew she'd said this over and over, to hear herself say it, to make herself believe. "He was dead for a week, and the animals got to him."

Outside the funeral home, dark and air-conditioned, the shock of Indian summer. Squinting against the sunshine, squeezing into limousines, avoiding the flash of cameras, we caravan back to Saddle River for the buffet in the barn.

There is fruit everywhere because this is what people (Jews?) do, I've discovered, they send fruit. Huge baskets weighty with waxy apples and globular grapes and willful bananas that *will* ripen too quickly or not at all at their own discretion, boxes of Carr's water crackers and chocolate-coated biscotti that'll break your teeth, packed with bright-green confetti or raffia that leaves a trail of dust across the counter.

My stepmother, behind sunglasses, actually extends her hand to stop my approach, avoids my eyes. We've not yet spoken. I appeal to Iris, her sister, who insists I must stay in touch with Noel.

"You must help each other through all this," she says, almost pleading.

What a crock, I can't help thinking at the time.

When Noel finally does speak to me, sedated, no doubt, with a drink in one hand, and a paper plate in the other, she stares hard into my face with unblinking eyes. We are both of us brittle—you could snap off our heads like dying geraniums—trying to be cordial in spite of the lack of genuine warmth between us.

"He loved you, he always told me he loved you," I stumble. Thirty-seven years later, here I am, such an idiot, still trying to win her approval.

"Well, I guess he must have, I mean look at his will. It's all left to me, isn't it? I'm his trustee, aren't I?" She searches my face for corroboration. "Did you know he was coming?" A crumb for me. "Did he tell you he was coming to Los Angeles the first of November? His ticket is on the desk in the bedroom."

"No. No, really? He was?" Oh God—oh Daddy—and I see him, grinning over his shoulder, letting the screen door slam behind him. *It's too much work to come here, too far from the course, Christ, it's exhausting.*

He'd been planning to come! Of course he had! He'd have

told me so, himself, the next time we spoke. The kids, I'm thinking, my babies, he couldn't stay away from my babies.

I am the tycoon's daughter, and I wonder, for a moment, if it's up to me to clear my plate. What's the protocol in a situation like this when your father is dead, and who is the caterer, and where is the busboy? My cousin Jason, Michael's son, relieves me, eases the plate out of my hands and puts it down on a table nearby, taking my arm, asking me if I wouldn't like to go for a walk. The brick steps down to the pool are every bit as elegant, every bit as grand as I remembered.

Out loud I'm working, I'm keeping the conversation alive, I'm trying to be gracious, I'm feeling responsible for entertaining this kind man, this cousin of mine whom I hardly know, who wants to be of comfort, and inside, I'm remembering and saying good-bye: to the pool where I'd lolled and lapped and played Marco Polo and pretended a thousand games (no diving board, not aesthetically correct), to the place where the brook used to run, where the blackberry bushes grew thick and high over our heads, to the apple tree, where I'd rested, painfully sunburned and fully clothed, my back against the trunk, waiting to recover and be allowed back in the water.

We wind up, finally, at the tennis courts, faded and stained, peeling in patches, although the white lines are freshly painted. Several years before my father had given up tennis for golf. When we asked him why, he said gravely, "Golf kills more time." He'd played tennis with Fred just once or twice since then. One evening he'd fed my self-taught scrapper of a husband a couple of martinis and some stuffed mushrooms and then challenged him to a match before dinner.

"You're a natural athlete," he'd said with grudging admiration. "A natural at everything you do, what I wouldn't give."

Now, as Jason and I step onto the court, Neil is standing at the net, swearing loudly and promising revenge to Geoffrey, who tells me again he cannot get over how much I am like my father, his dearest friend.

I wander away from them and back towards the house, passing a woman who looks to be my age; she is trim and pretty, and she's been crying. She nods at me and I realize in that instant she was his mistress. A golf pro, my father had spoken of her in passing but with quiet affection and respect; "A nice gal, very attractive, we've traveled the courses together." It was Gayle who'd told me the truth, just a few hours before. "Every time he buys that woman a plane ticket," she said, "Noel buys another horse."

In the house I continue my farewell tour until at last I find myself in the bedroom, where I have been going all along, to see for myself the round-trip ticket from Newark to LAX.

Later, when I'm filling a water glass at the kitchen sink, Aida asks, "Did you know he was coming to see you in November?"

I nod. And I drink the glass down.

17 | The Drama of the Not Particularly Gifted Child

My earliest memory, not even a memory anymore, a myth, a dream image described so many times it's gone out of focus and blurry on me: I'm not yet three but I'm already a swimmer, kicking my way across an enormous pool, holding onto a floating red barbell. If I shut my eyes tight I smell chlorine and Coppertone, sense the walls of the condominium shading one side of the pool. Am I wearing a bathing suit? Or just a pair of ruffled bottoms?

Inside the apartment there is a three-tiered table with colored glass animals arranged just so on each tier. Can it be I am allowed to play with them? There are women at the pool and in the house, women with brown skin, with freckles, with bleached hair, women with cookies and candies, there are old men with hairy ears and big bellies and wet kisses, there is my mother, in a paisley blouse. That was Miami, 1958, I learn when I am older, where my mother and I had moved to get a fast divorce.

In the wake of Watergate, my father, a Republican Party leader who made enemies in New Jersey when he threw the state to Nixon instead of Rockefeller in 1968, was accused of campaign fraud. He'd allegedly advised a supermarket chain to declare contributions tax deductible in a gubernatorial election four years before. He hired a celebrity defense attorney to represent him in the case, and between the two of them—arrogant, defiant, nothing remotely solicitous in their carriage (he was innocent, wasn't he?)—they alienated every court in New Jersey. My father served six months of a two-year sentence at Allenwood, a federal facility in Pennsylvania.

His mug shot from 1974, the year he went to prison, was all over the television that week in '97, the week he disappeared, even in Southern California. How unfair for the press to use that photo, grim and somehow implicating, when they might have chosen something a bit less sordid.

Late one evening, barely a week after his memorial service, full of despair, I call my mother.

"Mom, help me, I don't understand, I don't know why this happened."

A big pause, which I expect, since the cry is rhetorical, since there can't possibly be any definitive answer. But my mother steps into an omniscient role as if I wasn't a grown woman with children of my own, as if I was a child wailing in the dark.

"There are reasons," she says in a low voice, which is no comfort at all. "We can talk about the reasons if you want," she adds.

But I haven't called her less than a week after his body was found to hear her tell me his end had been in any way reasonable. Like the child in the dark, I'd wanted what? For her to tell me that everything would be all right in the morning? What?

I hear in her voice that she is helpless, too, that she doesn't understand what I need.

"How can I help you?" she asks, and I can't answer.

It will be months, even years, before I understand that she is only a mortal just like me, locked in her own psyche, forced to negotiate the world within the bounds of her own emotional experience, which includes mothering, of course, but which has very little to do with the super-mother myth that we have created together over the last forty years.

A few days later she calls to ask how I am.

"Terrible," I tell her. I am miserable, depressed, beyond sad.

"Really?" she asks, surprised. "Because I'm all right, I really am."

"As well you should be," I counter. "You divorced the guy thirty-seven years ago."

"Dinah," she says, all indignation, "I lived with the man, I had a child with him."

Oh Mom, I want to say, *that's just it, don't you see? That's me! I'm the child!*

Over a year later, the two of us sitting side by side in her psychiatrist's office for the sake of what will turn out to be her abbreviated foray into therapy, she will sob, "I'm sorry for you, so sorry, but Dinah, it's not my fault, I didn't kill your father!"

Of course she didn't. But try as she might, she couldn't let me mourn him either.

A few weeks after the murder, rummaging through shoe-boxes crammed with playbills, birthday cards, photographs, and old postcards, I find a whole packet of letters my father wrote me from prison, letters I'd forgotten having ever received. I call my mother again to say I've found them, written in his shaky hand, letters from my father, see? *See, Mom? He thought about me, he loved me, I'm not making it up, I'm not inventing a relationship that didn't exist!* She's glad for me, she says carefully, she hopes they are a comfort. She urges me to focus on the living, there's so much to live for. *I know that! I know! I just wanted you to hear . . .* We hang up awkwardly, me, with my shoebox and eleven letters, each a half a page long, not quite illegible, my mother, stymied and stupefied. What use could the letters be to me now? Why did they matter? Did they really change the fact of who he was, or who I believed him to be?

Thanksgiving, 1997. My father has been dead for two months. My whole family has decided to rally around and support me through the holiday. They will come to Los Angeles for the holiday. But things quickly go sour. My mother freaks out because she isn't invited to a siblings-and-spouses-only dinner at a Mexican restaurant the Tuesday before. On Wednesday she drops groceries on the doorstep and drives away without coming in, although we'd planned, she and my sister and I, to cook together all afternoon. She threatens to get on a plane and fly back to New York. She didn't come all this way to be insulted. There's no fixing this situation, which is suddenly and completely all about her.

A year or so before, she'd sent me Alice Miller's *The Drama of the Gifted Child*, about children who accommodate narcissistic parents, with a note suggesting that the book would help me understand what it was to grow up in her shoes. My therapist said then I ought to write Alice Miller and let her in on the joke.

Thanksgiving dinner is hell. My mother arrives in a huff. She looks nobody in the eye. She is humming under her breath, always a sure sign of pending disaster. Before we eat, I toast them all, thank them for being with me, for helping me through this difficult time. My brother Andy rolls his eyes in embarrassment, my stepfather laughs nervously, and Joe abruptly changes the subject. I have invited one friend, who makes a point of letting me know she's turned down other invitations because I need her. "My God, Dinah," she observes the next day, "those people don't even *like* you." I can't know at the time that I will fall out of touch with this woman. I can't predict that my mother will tell me, years later, "It was *she* we didn't like!" In the moment my friend's perception—if stunning—seems valid to me, serves my sense of alienation and remove.

How do you fit in when you're taller than your stepfather? When you talk too much? When your mother singles you out as more gifted, less gifted, more able, less able, because you're not one of them? How do you fit in when you miss family trips and vacations and come home full of notions about swimming pools and tennis courts in the backyard? How do you fit in when you're the only one who celebrates Christmas? When your father is running for elective office, but you and he have different last names? How do you fit in when you remind everyone who ever knew anything about you that you are a product of the first marriage, the bad marriage, the marriage that shouldn't have been a marriage at all? And how do you fit in when everyone else would be just fine except they happen to be related to you and you happen to be related to the man in the mug shot? The man who was murdered? Shit, you see? You've gone and done it again. Ruined everything for everybody, just by virtue of belonging but not belonging.

Well, of course, they don't like me, why should they?

18 | October, 1998

Here's a confession—here's something I regret: I never visited
my father in prison.

"Maybe you'll be able to take a day before school starts to
come up and look around," my father wrote from Allenwood.
"It's a good education," he added.

Relentless Rose made plans to drive me from Pelham to
Montgomery, Pennsylvania, an easy overnight trip.

Then my mother got into it.

"I'll take her," she told Rose. "I'll take you," she told me. "If
anyone's taking you to that place, I am," she said.

A message came back to me from my father. Never mind
the visit, he'd see me soon enough. If my mother was bringing me, he didn't want me to come. That was all.

I was ashamed of my father. I was ashamed to be ashamed.
I was eighteen years old, a sophomore in college; I should
have known better. I should have been more loyal, more loving, more interested, at least, but I was embarrassed and pur-
posefully ignorant. Horrified and ill-apprised. In those days,
when I talked about my father, I was quick to mention his
position as an assistant secretary of state in Nixon's cabinet. I

was aware on some level that his sort of notoriety put me in a league with kids from a certain kind of society. No, I hadn't prepped, but my father was serving time in a facility for important, moneyed, corporate-type criminals.

I wanted it all to go away. I had no idea whether or not he was guilty. I hoped he wasn't, in spite of my mother's tacit opinion, but guilty or not I was sick to my stomach when I thought about him there, terrified to see him—what? Behind bars? In a uniform? I'd have gone if I had to, but my parents, between them, had given me the perfect out. I was grateful for the excuse: my mother wouldn't let me go without her, my father wouldn't see me if she was anywhere in the vicinity. I'd been saved.

What was that? I should have gone! I should have supported him! I should have behaved like a daughter!

We never spoke of it, my father and I. He only told me once, without looking at me, that whatever I thought about Noel, she'd stayed with him through tough times.

"She could have left," he said. "That time I was in prison, she was there with Neil once a week. She could have given up on me. It would have been easier on her. She stuck by me through it all."

It turns out there's no trial. The boys, all three minors when the crime was committed, have arranged to confess to kidnapping in a plea agreement and will be sentenced accordingly just over a year after my father's death.

Here's what's frustrating: nobody gets that I need to be in that courtroom.

My stepfather tells me he doesn't understand me, so I explain that my father would have wanted me there, would have demanded my presence, my loyalty, would have told me to stand up for him and be counted as his daughter.

"I don't believe that," says Ron.

He's convinced I'm wrong to go, misguided in my certainty that my father would have asked for me. He says they had private conversations; that he knew the man better than I think.

"Someday I will share with you," he adds before we hang up.

This response seems cruel and manipulative. I love this man, my stepfather, and I know he's attached to me, but *someday* he will share? Which day? When? What better time than now, now when I need to know everything about my father from anyone who will tell me; *And you*, I want to say to him, *Who raised me and did your best to love me as your own, why do you withhold from me now? Why do you want to take this away from me, this time when I wear my love for my father openly, my face like his my best offense, my only revenge, my badge of condemnation, why would you not have me look his killers in the eye and have them see me and know? He was my father—you stole my father from me— you stole his life from him.*

After I hang up the phone, I'm hot with resentment. I want so much for this other father to understand: in death I must acknowledge the relationship, embrace the man proudly and publicly; in death I'm justified in loving him without regard for you, without fear of hurting your feelings or losing your love.

I have asked to see the place where my father died and Uncle Michael has decided to come along. I sit in the middle of the backseat of the sedan—between Michael and Fred—with a dozen roses in my lap, closed, without thorns, without scent, purchased on the corner of Thirty-third and Lexington just before we were picked up by two plainclothes cops in a pale blue sedan. They are the ones who found my father and eventually, the teenagers who killed him.

"I don't understand why you want to be there," Michael had protested on the phone some days earlier, having learned I intended to fly east for the sentencing. "Is it some sort of vengeance you have in mind?"

Michael was the hippie, the flower child, the prodigal son. My father lost patience with Michael sometime in the '60s. His voice shook with anger when he spoke of his youngest brother, who'd eulogized him beautifully, nonetheless, the year before. This was the brother who'd announced that politicians were pigs when my Republican father was running for office. This was the brother who'd publicly advocated recreational drug use when my father was the head of International Drug Control under President Nixon (the bone of a title thrown him after he'd won Bergen County for Nixon in '68 but lost his own bid for the Senate in the following election). My father valued loyalty above all things. Loyalty was his measure of character and Michael had proved himself disloyal, unworthy of my father's attention or regard.

On the telephone with me, Michael had gone on to say that vengeance was no answer, that rehabilitation was possible, that I mustn't expect justice, nor should I take comfort in ruined lives.

I'd cut him off during that conversation, impatient to explain that I had to be there to bear witness, to show myself; the killers needed to see me to understand that they'd murdered my father and my children's grandfather, not just *some old man*. He was connected and he was loved.

Michael was silent for a moment, and I knew I'd hit a nerve. He'd understood, he'd heard me.

When we talk again, on our way up Riverside Drive to the place where my father died, he tells me I've helped him. He's the designated speaker for the family the following day, the day of the sentencing, and my words have allowed him to focus better on what he wants to say.

The detectives drive us through Washington Heights, pointing out the landmarks, describing the community, explaining that the young people here have nothing to live for, no way to get ahead, no sense of the American Dream except that somebody else has it and they don't and, Christ, it would be so easy to get a piece of it without working all that hard, and working hard never got anybody anywhere so far as they can see.

"Not that we condone that," one of the cops explains. "Plenty of ghetto cultures don't subscribe to that kind of thing, but these kids, they got no sense of the value of life, they see a rich, old man like your father, they figure he has plenty, enough for them and way more than he deserves so why not get what they got coming."

Michael nods with empathy.

"But he did what they wanted, he gave them what they asked for . . ." I trail off, and then, "I just don't believe it, it doesn't make any sense, why'd he get in the car with them, why did he do what they said?"

My father, 6' 2", maybe 220 pounds, and three punks under 5' 8", two of them not yet eighteen, slight, Spanish-speaking, the sort of people my father didn't see, the sort he'd brush away like bugs, how come he gave in?

"You don't know what you'd do if a gun was pointed at you," is always the answer, and it always seems wrong to me, completely out of character; I will never understand.

Somebody tell me: two cars pulled over on the West Side Highway. A tall, older white man, and two young Latinos, short and dark, standing by the side of the road. Didn't anyone notice at eleven o'clock in the morning? And when did he know he was in trouble? And why didn't he ask for help? At the bank. In the parking lot. On the phone. Why didn't he smash the car into the tollbooth? Drive it down the ravine. Why did he get in and get out when they told him to? Why did he follow them down the embankment? What was he thinking while they debated killing him, in Spanish, in the back of his car? And when he was dying, what went through his mind? Did he think about us, his wife, his daughter, his son, his grandchildren? Was he all of his sixty-five years, or was he a boy on a bicycle in the driveway in Ridgewood? A player in the outfield straining to catch a fly ball? Married to my mother with me in his arms; married to my stepmother with his son in his lap. Or was he in the moment and did he know that his life had been stolen from him with a pocketknife?

The picture in the *Bergen County Record* showed a bunch of men in uniform, hoisting a long stretcher, a lumpy silhouette covered in a yellow tarp being pulled out of the ravine with ropes and pulleys, no other way to get him out, it was so steep.

I close my eyes, and I imagine my father in his linen blazer and his wrinkle-free khakis, negotiating the path in his dress shoes, and I pray he thought they would leave him there and make their escape; I pray he believed they would tie him to a tree and blindfold him and hike away, nothing more; I pray he swore to himself under his breath, wondering how the hell he was going to climb out of the gully, never knowing, never believing one kid would drop a boulder on his head and the other would charge him with a knife, cut his arms and his hands, his neck, his chest, his face until he couldn't fight anymore. They left him with his watch and his money clip, they left him there, in the blazing September sun, in the downpour that came afterwards, and they boasted about their new clothes, hubcaps, motorcycle, to the rest of the neighborhood. *What did he think?* What did he remember as his life proverbially passed before his eyes?

I throw roses that will never open into the ravine, and they disappear in a thicket of ivy and tall grass and weeds, so overgrown there isn't a path anymore. There's no way I can see to climb down to the place where a tattered strip of orange tape hangs from the trunk of a birch, a year and a month after the murder.

"What is that?" I ask the cops who stand waiting respectfully apart, not speaking, straight-legged, hands clasped together behind their backs. Waiting for me to do what? To pray? To cry? To throw myself over the side of the guardrail? *What?* I have no idea what to do with myself.

One of them answers, "From the crime scene."

He is young, maybe thirty, blue-eyed, snub-nosed, short, fine brown hair, and an open, Irish face. His partner is older, has a couple of kids, but this one isn't married yet. "Guess I'm not really looking," he says. He tells us his dad, who is also dead, was a cop before him.

"Did you find my father?" It's all I can do not to tug on his sleeve. "Can you tell me—can you tell me how you found him?"

"I did," he answers. "I found him down there, in the fetal position, facing out over the river. . . . I swear he could have been looking at his restaurant when he took his last breath. You can see it down there—the ferryboat—you can see it just perfect, sitting there on the other side of the river."

He continues low-voiced and deliberate, "I put in the call, you know, and then I just sat down there with him, on a rock over there, you can't see it now, it's so overgrown, but I sat with him for, I don't know, maybe a half an hour. It was strange thinking he died looking over at his own business—so close to here and all—but he's in a better place now, though. That's what I believe, ma'am. He's in a better place."

19 | Mementos

I think of life as vertical—an upward climb, no going back—but what if it happened on the horizontal axis? What if it were possible to visit any dot on the graph? What if each dot stood for a moment suspended in space, and what if there were a secret to reentry, to how and where to find access? Suppose the answer was a photograph. Suppose you could step into an image, a moment captured, and suppose it continued and continued and continued somewhere somehow for all time.

There's a picture I love; blown up from a Polaroid and not especially good, but there he is, my father, in a suit and tie, and I'm standing in front of him in a plaid jumper, nine or ten, red tights and Mary Janes, convulsed in giggles, pigeon-toed. He's laughing, too, tickling me under the arms.

And then there's the five-by-eight in the silver frame in front of the lamp on my desk: Eliza can't be more than four years old. She's decked out for Halloween in a shiny dress with puffed sleeves and an oversized tiara, hands clasped before her, staring off into the distance, listening intently to Pop, who holds her wand and leans into her ear, telling her something important and magical.

One more image that is all about my father; a panoramic photo in a long rectangular frame on top of my dresser. Eliza, six, in a pink bathing suit, appears to be skipping up the sand from the shoreline on a flat expanse of beach, while Jake stands braced against the oncoming tide, knees bent, arms spread wide, wind blowing up under his oversized turquoise trunks. My father took this picture in the summer of 1996 with a brand-new camera he'd bought for just that occasion. Every time I see it, every morning when I take a clean pair of socks out of the middle drawer and put them on before I trudge upstairs to make the coffee and pack school lunches, I'm reminded of him, squinting into the lens, focusing on his grandchildren.

"He saw this," I tell myself. "This is what he saw."

The morning of the sentencing, Fred and I hail a cab on Lexington Avenue and leave New York City for New Jersey to face relatives who'd rather forget about me now that my father is dead. At odds with Paul and Gayle over matters of Nelson's last will and testament, we are not invited to stay at the house this time. Instead we're lodged in the Gramercy Park Hotel— quirky, worn at the edges—sleeping under a polyester quilt (it shines), and showering under an ambivalent showerhead, now hot, now strong, now cold, now a trickle.

We stop in front of the courthouse in Trenton and eat an English muffin in a dark, empty diner across the street. The bathroom has one of those toilets with the tank on the wall and a chain to flush it and no toilet paper, just a stack of brown paper towels that smell like cardboard on the back of the seat. I'm wearing a black suit that I bought the day before and wondering if it will be hard to wear again. I'd been warned that the green suit would always be my funeral costume, but I'd managed to wear it a dozen times since. This suit, too, I'm resolved, will have a life hereafter. All of my clothes belong to a woman whose father was murdered; one outfit isn't more cursed than another.

The muffin doesn't help. I'm queasy, hands clammy, as anxious about confronting my relatives as I am about seeing the families of the boys in the courtroom and the boys themselves. No, I'm more fearful of my relations. So unnerved am I by the idea of seeing my father's brothers, wife, and son, I have to remind myself over and over I've come to look his killers in the face; the rest is incidental.

We're ushered into a conference room to meet with the prosecutors and my uncles and their wives before we file inside the courtroom all together. I'm armed with photos of my children, whom I still want my uncles to embrace a year after the murder and in spite of Paul's anger over the estate.

"Very pretty, very grown up," says my stepmother, of my daughter. Noel is wearing velvet slacks, a fuzzy green sweater and enormous sunglasses. She passes the pictures to Paul, who looks hard at Jake in his baseball uniform.

"That's Nelson," he says. "It's uncanny, Gayle." He pushes the snapshot across the table to his wife. "Look at this, will you?"

"Uh huh," she murmurs. "Isn't he big?" And she hands the pictures back without looking at me.

Before we go in, Noel gives me a gold cardboard box, taped shut, inside a small shopping bag. A month or so before, when I knew we were traveling to New York for the sentencing, I'd called Michael to ask where my father was buried.

"He wasn't," he said when he got back to me. "Noel has the ashes, she'll give you a third of them when she sees you."

What third of the man do I have in this box (the other two thirds presumably residing in Saddle River, New Jersey), and would my father have minded being divvied up into portions? Before I put it on the floor between my feet, I notice the small brown bag is actually from the Body Shop.

In the courtroom, before he imposes his sentences, the judge hears various motions from the defense and opposing arguments from the prosecution. Finally he recognizes Michael, who approaches the rostrum to make his statement.

"We recognize the niceties, and we respect them and appreciate them," says my uncle, with regard to the reduced charges of the plea agreement. "But as a family member of the victim of the crime . . . we'd like the Court to know that, for us, it is murder . . . to us now, not as lawyers, but as the survivors, our brother, father, husband, and son was murdered. . . . If any one of these persons had said to the other, 'Let's rob and kill our brother, our father, a member of our family,' we assume that they would have resisted that; that their conscience would have made them recognize the outrageous thing that was being suggested here. . . . And so we feel that one of the incapacities that they suffer from is a lack of awareness of the humanity of the individual . . . whose life they took.

"And so my only purpose here this morning is to, by introducing us to the Court, respectfully, that they should through that process learn that he, too, has a family. . . . They scarred and injured those whom he was integrated with as a family member, certainly—I hope they appreciate—as much as I hope they are integrated in their own families."

This is what Michael has gleaned from my determination to be in this courtroom; the men who did this thing must see us as one, connected together and individually to the man they killed.

"I am, sir, Michael Gross," he continues. "They murdered my brother. And that gentleman at the end of the row is Paul Gross, and they murdered his brother."

He points us out, son, daughter and mother of his grandchildren, finally Noel, my father's widow.

"They need to recover an awful lot of humanity before they can really understand the enormity of their conduct . . . so that we can begin to feel unburdened of some of the pain that we feel, because part of it is our inability to deal with how, why, they killed him after they took his money.

"I close with one word, which I am told they heard him say to them. They're killing him, and he spoke one word to them, several times, they said. At the scene, while they beat him, while they cut him, he said the word that I convey to this Court in consideration of its responsibility to impose sentence on them. He said to them: enough."

The boys—brown-skinned, wiry and slight—claim not to speak English fluently, so their attorneys speak for them. One lawyer, in his appeal for leniency, for a "downward departure" in the sentencing, has already stated how disturbing it is that his client appears to be "a very ordinary young man. . . . That someone who seems so ordinary can be involved in something so extraordinary leads a person to wonder what the capacities of human beings really are." Now, for the last time, the defense points to mitigating circumstances: lack of resources, lack of education, cooperation with the law, admission of guilt, and professed contrition.

When at last they give their own statements, the first two, the killers, look at their feet and mumble in Spanish, an awkward hum underscoring the translator, whose tenor is flat and unfaltering. They speak quickly, without remorse it seems, while their families sob aloud on the other side of the room.

The third, who is slightly older, who drove the second car but did not hurt my father, looks at us and speaks in English. He is impassioned and digressive, as though he knows that when he finishes speaking it will truly be over, he will not have another chance: "I wish I could have done what I wanted to do now. I tried, think about it from time to time, I can't. . . . As much as I want to make a difference, all I can do is hope for the best for you. . . . I heard that his daughter was the one who was hurt the most. . . . I ask her to take some time to come to speak to me personally. Any questions she wants to ask me, if I can answer, I will answer."

I can't swallow and his face is a blur across the room. I know I'm breathing too hard from the way Fred squeezes my hand, and I blink furiously, but I can't bring the room into focus.

I'm holding my little brown bag with both hands as we leave the courtroom. Towards the end of his introductions, Michael had actually referred to my package, my box of remains.

"By an irony, not planned, Nelson Gross's ashes are in this courtroom today," he'd said.

Theatrical, yes, but ill-advised, since this last has the reporters on me and my treasure like flies on relish, as soon as we leave the courthouse for a press conference.

Outside, before we meet the press, a young social worker from the DA's office with heavily lined eyes and a stud in her nose touches my arm and asks softly, "Can I take that for you? Until afterwards, I mean?"

I hand her the bag. I wish she would be my best friend, would come for dinner, would play with my children, but I know that after today I'll never see her again.

The next morning I will wait for a train in Grand Central Station, because my mother, having demanded equal time, wants me to meet with her and her therapist in Riverdale. I will buy the *New York Times* and we'll be on the cover of the metro section, Noel and I. She, thin-lipped, will look especially grim, while I, gaze lowered, will appear to be agonized, when, in fact, we were shaking with stifled laughter at having foiled the press at the very last moment.

But during the press conference we sober up fast. Michael, leaning on a cane, looks suddenly old and gray and small to me. And where, oh where, is Nelson, shouldn't he be here? Shouldn't he speak for himself? What would he look like today if he were alive?

Afterward, when the social worker returns the bag to me, she delivers a letter from the third boy, whose own father had been shot to death several years before. According to the confessions, he'd tried to persuade his friends to let my father live, moments before they forced him down the ravine.

"What if he was your *father*?" he'd asked them.

His penmanship, in blue ink on lined white paper, is mostly careful, printed in lowercase, some of the small letter *i*'s dotted with circles, other letters capitalized at random having nothing to do with his equally arbitrary punctuation. The letter begins with a prayer for my good health. Then the writer identifies himself—his name is Tony Estevez—if I'm wondering, he says, he's the one who could have saved my father. His own father left when he was a year old, he confides, and didn't recognize Tony when they met again ten years later. The very same evening, his father was shot in the head and killed for money, just like mine. He has only ever known his mother, who suffers from asthma. He doesn't remember, he admits, what it's like to have a father, but he's sorry for me, and certain, too, that I won't believe his sympathy is sincere.

The handwriting becomes more erratic now, subjects and verbs don't agree, the tenses are inconsistent and Tony forgets to punctuate altogether, remembering his confusion and fear on the day of the murder. He swears he tried to stop his friends from going through with it, and he reminds me he has no reason to lie. He's not asking for freedom, he pleads, only forgiveness.

Tony insists he's never done anything wrong before; he's only been a comfort to his mother and younger siblings, for whom he provides. He bemoans this terrible mistake, but he was frightened! Afraid to do the right thing, to notify the police! If he could bring the man back to life he would, and he prays that God will forgive him.

In closing, he asks me to visit. He has a heart, he writes. He isn't like the others; he understands my pain. He wants me to know him for who he really is.

In the first few moments after I read the letter, I waver, wonder out loud what to do and how to feel. Fred, reading over my shoulder, reminds me that this boy took his share of the money, left my father to die in the tall weeds by the riverbank, neglected to come forward until he had no other choice.

"You don't have to answer, Dine," he says quietly.

The letter is carefully folded and eventually stashed away in the big brown file with the torn clasp.

A different person would respond. Would find forgiveness in mutual understanding and acceptance. Would write letters of support, send money to his family, make certain his ailing mother received medical care and that his younger siblings stayed in school. A different person, someone with religion, would transform these random events with spiritual meaning, would take solace in bridging the culture gap. A different person, someone with faith in the big picture, would mine this tragedy for epiphany and hope.

Not I. Not this person. This person I am cannot dig that deep, nor cross that gulf. This person would rather pretend that other person, the person who's going to prison, doesn't exist.

No point in visiting Tony Estevez—I haven't an ounce of missionary in me—I don't want to comfort him and he will be no more comfort to me than is anyone else who has witnessed or survived a tragedy. My grief is specific and unfathomable and mine alone. I resent anyone, prophet or victim in his own right, who thinks he can make sense of my father's death. Anyone who talks about universal truths and reasons is at best a well-intentioned bore, and it's all I can do in the face of that brand of sympathy—all-knowing, all-accepting—to keep my eyes from glazing over.

Poor Tony Estevez. Nearly six years later, the way he's

signed his name in cursive above the printed letters, deliberate but wobbly, reminds me of Jake. I imagine Tony hunched over the page, as I've seen my son hunched over his homework so many times, pencil gripped so tight in his fist that his fingers cramp. Jake, entirely focused on doing his best, on pleasing me. Jake, who, at ten years old, wakes up happy most mornings and eager to get on with his day. Oh, I'm sorry for Tony Estevez, and I'm sorry for his mother. I wonder fleetingly what sort of son, husband, father he might have been and might yet be after he serves his seventeen years and returns to Washington Heights, a man in his thirties. I wonder, just for a moment, if he hates me now: such a heartfelt bid for my attention and no response at all, ever, from me. Even so, I've no investment in assuaging his guilt, absorbing his pain, etching a connection between the two of us. He can't bring me closer to my father and, tortured though he may be, his remorse is of no consequence to me now.

20 | Messages Received

Early on Jake has a nightmare. It's the night after the night I learned my father was missing. I don't know it, but he's been dead for nearly three days. His body lies on a riverbank in the rain, curled onto its side, covered in dirt and blood, and by this time he's long gone.

People say children are intuitive, and they know when something is up, and I'm sure they're right. How could my children not have felt my apprehension, my fear, my dread, my anxiety during that first thirty-six hours? But we were careful, and we didn't let on. We kept the truth from them because we didn't know what the truth would turn out to be. I may have been snappish, tense, overwhelmed, but I never even hinted that my mood had anything to do with their grandfather. So when Jake with the big heart, Jake who is innately spiritual and helplessly connected to the universe, Jake, who at four is my father's only grandson, wakes in the middle of the night weeping inconsolably, and tells us he has dreamed that bad men have taken *his* daddy away, I am sure he's had a ghostly visitor.

We soothe him, we sing to him, we hold him until he falls asleep, we tiptoe downstairs to our bed, pull up the comforter, and I tell Fred, "Well, he's dead, he must be. I mean he must have been here, visiting Jake, telling Jake good-bye."

My father was crazy for Jake. We all knew it, even Eliza. Once, during a visit, she cried from the backseat of the car that Pop liked Jake better than her, and I, distraught, climbed over the front seat to hold her and explain that Pop loved her very much, he just wasn't all that good at showing it. He was gruff, sometimes, I explained, brusque, easier with boys than with girls, but he loved her, I promised he did.

When I told a friend about it, she said, "Dinah, don't be silly, she's fine, he's her grandfather, not her father, she has two wonderful parents who adore her, she isn't you, don't endow her with your feelings."

My son was cheery and funny from the start. He was solidly built and darker than his sister, with those up-slanting eyes. I wanted to think my father saw himself in Jake and figured this time we'd get it right.

In the meanwhile I'm jealous, too—jealous of my son's night visitor—until I start to have dreams of my own:

My father is a scarecrow in a tuxedo, hanging by his suit jacket from the ceiling at a masquerade ball, silent as a mannequin in the static of smoke and party noise, he's dead, swinging from the rafters, like a huge piñata.

I'm buckled in the backseat, and my father is driving me to an audition. He makes an illegal U-turn, gets me there just in time, waves me off in the rearview mirror, doesn't speak but it's understood that he'll wait in the car. I'm wearing a kilt, knee-socks, and penny loafers, not at all self-conscious even though I'm a woman over forty.

I'm at a funeral, somebody's funeral, and my father is there but he hovers, ethereal, a few feet off the ground, and says nothing.

My father's will has been read, his estate divided. I've been bequeathed fifty thousand sliced onions.

My father is being led away from a town meeting, pulled from the hall by bad guys. I race to catch up with him and he stops, hugs me longer and closer than I remember him ever doing in life, kisses me, tells me it's all right, it's just business.

I am trying to steal a stack of photos from my stepmother's store (no, she doesn't have one, only in the dream) and in one of the photos, my father smiles and winks at me, although he's dead. He moves in the picture, nods to reassure me, urging me on, telling me it's all right to steal, to slip his likeness from the stack on the table and into the front of my jacket, because this particular image belongs to me.

A documentary about my father's family. Three actors play the three sons. There's a drug connection, a crime, something bad, something dirty. I stand outside the cameras, watching my father— a young actor who is not my father—as if watching him will make him notice me. No one acknowledges my presence here, nobody cares, until a reporter just a few feet away asks, Isn't that Nelson's daughter? I start to cry and I am instantly ashamed. Using grief to get attention. Using this disaster, making use of it; what is that?

The best dream of all: *my father and I are watching a show in an old Broadway theater, worn red velvet seats and carved, gold-painted columns, but when the curtain falls at the end of the play, the seat beside me is suddenly empty. The orchestra strikes up "Shall We Dance" and Anna appears with the rest of the cast to take her bows without the King, because the King is dead.*

When he's dead in the dreams, my father's head bobs in and out of rooms like an odd note on a player piano. Or like a buoy in the bay.

But sometimes he appears full-bodied and all of a piece, wearing an overcoat, standing beside his car, waiting to pick me up and take me somewhere, home, maybe, wherever that is. I'm packing in the dreams, endlessly packing, and I know I'm dreaming. I want to wake up, to stop packing, to stop finding items of clothing I didn't know belonged to me, that have to be stowed somewhere, not enough space, not enough luggage. This is the sort of dream that continues in spite of inter-ruptions—that picks up where it left off—that goes on *all night long*, even if you get up to go to the bathroom or to take a sip of water. So I know that I'm dreaming, which is exhausting on some level, because I'm not entirely submerged, no, I'm try-ing to negotiate a shift, anything, a different kind of torture, but no more packing please, because the packing, I tell my-self sternly, is just a dream. What I don't know, what I don't remember until I wake up, is that my father—waiting there for me and my umpteen overstuffed duffel bags, leaning against his big sedan and gnawing on the side of his thumb, silent, al-ways silent in the dreams—is actually dead.

Here's the big fear: irrational, narcissistic, yes, and rooted in superstition and the suspicion that events are not random at all. Or that they are. First off, I assure myself that nothing else can happen to me or mine. We've been hit once and hit hard and what are the chances that one family would suffer more than one tragedy? Well, look at the Kennedys, you moron. The fact is, bad things can happen to the same people over and over again, no rhyme or reason and nobody keeping cosmic score. And if the whole scenario is more (or less) mysterious and incomprehensible than it seems? If there *is* life after death? If there *are* angry ghosts? What if my father will not rest until he takes one of us along with him? What if he wants Jake? It is Jake I fear for, it is Jake I assume he'll demand as a sacrifice or just for his own entertainment. You leave him alone, I insist in my head, when Jake runs a high fever, gets a weird stomach flu, takes a scary tumble on the playground.

The summer after my father's death, when Jake is five, he gets separated from us on a beach in Carpinteria, a little town just south of Santa Barbara, where we've stopped to visit friends for the day. One minute he's beside me, the next he's gone. Fred and I stand up to our knees in the surf, shouting his name, scanning the beach, the waves.

"Somebody help me, somebody help!" I scream.

Out of nowhere, a woman, blond is all I can remember, comes toward me, holding my baby's hand in hers.

"Is this your boy?" she asks me.

Jake is crying convulsively, and I drop to my knees in the sand to hold him.

"I'm here, honey, Mommy's here," I say out loud, but in my head I am shaking my fist. "You can't have him," I say to my father. "He's mine, not yours."

This is ridiculous, I know. My father is dead. He has no posthumous plans for my children. He's dust, or if he isn't, well, then, he wishes them well, he wishes them long, happy lives and infinite good fortune. He would only protect them, if he could, keep them safe and happy and well.

When I look up to thank the blond angel (and you have to wonder for a moment, don't you, who sent her?), she's disappeared in the crowd.

21 | Nelson and Leah

I call my mother on her sixty-seventh birthday with the *Los Angeles Times* on the table in front of me, open to the horoscopes. I explain that Sydney Omarr is dead, but how lucky for us all he was so far ahead of schedule, his predictions and insights continuing to appear on the back page of the calendar section for our general edification and revelation even now.

"You'll have a wonderful day," I inform her, "and listen up, Ma, there's something about how former lovers will be in touch."

"Hmmpf," she pronounces, almost embarrassed, and she adds, "God, I wonder if any of them are even alive."

She wasn't always sixty-seven, overweight and gray with bad knees and feet. Although she will always be beautiful, my mother was glamorous and desirable, too, easily the most compelling person in the room straight through middle age. A connoisseur of music, art, and food, she wore a French twist and designer suits, sheer gray hose and Ferragamo t-straps. She had a life—a career—exclusive of her children and her marriages, too. (We've commiserated over lost youth, my mother and I—it gets my goat when she lumps us together—but from her point of view we are barely a generation apart.)

"Well, anyway," I say, "happy birthday, Ma. Let me know if you hear from anyone interesting."

It occurs to me when I hang up that my mother is older now than my father was when he was killed. Odd to think about that. Odd when we out-distance people who were always ahead of us. The idea that I could bump into my father somewhere somehow a few decades from now, and I'd be the old one. How would he know me? How would he recognize me at eighty or ninety, stooped, wizened, wrinkled, twenty, thirty years his senior?

It was, it is, in spite of my ambivalent self, a source of pride for me that I am like my father. My stepfather is a small man. I was taller than he before I finished high school, and I held my breath (no girl wants to be bigger than her father and her brothers) until Joe and Andy, my siblings from the second marriage, grew taller than I. Lucky for me—eager as I was to be assimilated most of the time—we all looked enough like my mother to be members of the same family.

My mother is the one who could have been a movie star. The story is that a talent scout spied her in the lobby of her building when she was a little girl. If my grandparents had allowed it, she'd have gone off to Hollywood and woe to Elizabeth Taylor; *National Velvet* would have been a whole other movie. She had the coloring, the bones. White skin, amber eyes, wavy black hair. She and my father looked alike—exotic, striking, athletic, all-American Jews—celebrities at Teaneck High School, both of them, but four years apart. She was dubbed "brilliant" and "a raven-haired beauty" in the yearbook; he was a football star, admitted across the boards to the Ivy League. He thumbed his nose at Harvard, where his own father earned two degrees, and went off to Yale when she was a high school freshman. Uncle Paul, though, four years his junior, was in my mother's class. She was cheerleading when Nelson came back to a high school football game in the fall of 1952, his last year in New Haven. That night Paul called my mother to ask her out on a date with his big brother the Yalie.

"Does he have a tongue?" Leah wanted to know.

She married him the following year, when she was eighteen and a freshman at Sarah Lawrence, where she went, instead of Radcliffe or Vassar or Wellesley (she could have gone anywhere), so they could be together while he studied law at Columbia.

So she was the beauty with no heir apparent; none of her children, not I, nor the others from the second marriage, ever quite measured up. Her younger sister, my Aunt Abby, has a very handsome son who makes my mother go misty because maybe he resembles her a little. My features, she's intimated over the years, are a bit less fine; I'm bigger, broad-shouldered, with long toes like fingers. The Grosses, she always said, are good peasant stock (sturdy, tough, long-lived, and a little coarse) and physically, she's marveled often enough, I am a Gross through and through.

Well, I wanted to look like my mother, what little girl doesn't, even if her mother isn't an acknowledged beauty? (My own daughter often asks if she will look like me when she grows up, and when an innocent bystander says how much she resembles her father, she proclaims, not a little indignant, that our baby pictures, hers and mine, are identical.) Still, I wasn't sorry to look like him. There was my link, my connection, my validation, my proof! I had so little of him, I saw so little of him; he was tall, handsome, larger than life, a politician, a celebrity, even, and I was very obviously his little girl.

Poolside at the Beverly Hills Hotel, Nelson showed me his will. I was very pregnant for the first time, which means it had to be autumn, 1989.

"I wrote it myself," said my father. "Neil gets the house, because that's where he grew up. And he gets a little more here and there because I raised him. You've always had another family, Dinah," he reminded me.

"Now," he said, jabbing at the document with his shaking index finger, "do you know how much this estate is worth to you? Read it carefully. Let me know what you think."

"I think I'm better off if you stay alive," I was flipping pages. "I don't inherit anything until I'm fifty-five—at which point my baby will be twenty-two, just out of college, for God's sake—so don't die whatever you do because I might need a little help with higher education."

He chuckled. Little did he know he'd broken every tax law ever written with this will, this long, involved treatise of which he was inordinately proud. Little did he know.

"Now look, Dinah, whatever you name this baby," he was squinting up at the sun reflected off the salmon-colored facade of the hotel above us, "you'd better not name it after anyone in your mother's family.

"You never took my name, you never did. You insulted me. And now I'm asking you not to name this child after the Bingers."

"I won't, Dad." I tried unsuccessfully to catch his eye. "I promise I won't."

One night, during one of his visits, we got a sitter and my father took us to Patina on Melrose in Hollywood, where we ate Caesar salad with wafer-thin croutons and seared tuna and tarte tatin with homemade vanilla ice cream.

I asked him to tell me what happened between them.

"I don't talk about those things. It's the past. You don't need to know about it."

"I know she had an affair." Very bold.

He glanced up. He looked at his food.

"I know she had an abortion."

Pause. "Not my child."

"I know that, too." *Please, Dad, tell me your side.*

"I begged her to come back. She betrayed me, and she took you from me."

I asked if it was true that he'd wanted to borrow money from her father after they'd separated, that it was because of the money that he'd tried to reconcile. He stared at me. I'd gone too far. When he spoke, so low I had to lean forward to hear him, his voice caught in his throat.

"I loved you, Dinah. Who do you think changed those diapers? Do you think it was your mother? I loved you."

I knew he believed what he was saying whether or not it was true.

I told my mother what he said about naming the baby. She and I were deep in the corners of my custom-made couch, upholstered in designer fabric, the one that she ordered for me after I got my first big television job; Fred sat across from us in a rocking chair we'd picked up at a flea market that afternoon.

"You know what I think?" She nodded her head slowly. She was pensive, compassionate. "I think that's a bid for you to name this baby for him. And you should, Dinah, you should give the baby his name—as a middle name, you know—it'd work for a boy or a girl. It'd please him so much."

Her generosity was stunning. And persuasive.

But later, when Fred and I discussed it, he objected. He wasn't naming his son or daughter for my father. It just didn't feel right to him.

"Let's not be bullied," he said.

This was, after all, before we had the kids, before they brought out a kinder, gentler Nelson, before my father began to visit us without his wife, before we found an intimacy that only his grandchildren could have facilitated.

So weeks later I had my mother on the telephone about one thing or another and I told her, "By the way, Mom, we're not going to name the baby after Nelson. Fred feels uncomfortable about it. He just doesn't want to, not even as a middle name."

"What are you talking about?"

"You know. How you said we should name the baby after my father."

"Dinah, I never said such a thing! How could you think that? How could I condone your naming a baby after that man? Don't you realize how hurtful that would be to me and Daddy?"

And I knew that she believed what she was saying whether or not it was true.

22 | Coming and Going

"They didn't want you around all that much."

This from my mother, in response to my asking what the legal agreement was with regard to visitation: I can't remember how often I was there. Two weeks in the winter, two weeks in the summer, isolated weekends, was that it?

"You were never there for two weeks in the winter—you spent school vacations with him—never two weeks at a time.

"Ruth didn't want us around either," she adds.

She's talking about her own father's second wife, whom he married when she was in her thirties, long after she'd moved out of her parents' house, after she'd been married twice and borne four children, but if I stop her now, if I ask her if she believes there's any kind of equation here, she'll wonder out loud if every conversation must be only all about me.

I must be careful to stay neutral, not to appear wounded or doubtful as to her version of events and not to diminish her own alienation if that's what she wants to talk about. First off, any hurt on my part and we'll spiral off on a jag about what is and isn't an honest conversation and her having to censor herself to spare my feelings. Second, she must be right. He didn't want me around. And considering how little I remember, I mustn't have spent all that much time with him. All of this was the fabric of my mother's adult life; she's bound to remember better than I.

"It was a pain in the ass, frankly. I was juggling a family—I had three other kids—he'd decide he wanted you or he didn't at the last minute."

There are adults who like little kids and those who don't. The ones who do usually like children in direct proportion to the way those children reflect their own talents and inclinations. Truth be known I don't have much patience for other people's children. Children are mostly uninteresting except to professionals—teachers, counselors, pediatricians, and their own parents—and even then hours, days, weeks, months, hell, years go by that are deadly boring, only worth remembering as circuitous channels toward various rites of passage. As a child I couldn't have been all that interesting to my father; he wasn't consumed with my day to day progress, and my hour to hour needs were a jolt to his system when I descended on the scene with all my conscious and unconscious demands.

Of course there are adults who have the gift, who actually like kids, who have not forgotten how to play, who are endlessly tolerant and fascinated. My stepfather is one of these, as was his mother before him (a schoolteacher in the Bronx who brought a vat of oatmeal to work in the mornings because she knew her students weren't getting a decent breakfast), as are at least two of his children, Andy and Jill.

Around the time I learned about sex, I asked my mother if Ron had been upset to discover, on their wedding night, that she wasn't a virgin. She burst out laughing which, at age ten, I didn't understand, even when she explained that they'd met on a blind date, that Ron knew from the start she was divorced with a daughter.

The story goes he couldn't wait to have kids of his own and

would have had more if my mother had agreed. As it was, they had two boys, Joe and Andy, two years apart, Joe just eleven months after their September wedding which made me nearly five when he was born. Then Jill, nearly seven years after Andy, *an unexpected pleasure*, they called her, but my mother cried through that pregnancy, still resents the almost twenty years she gave to child care, diapers, mashed bananas, pushing swings, and tying shoes. My mother didn't have the gift, but she was smart enough the second time around to marry a man who did.

My daughter, at ten, is flying by herself for the first time, to spend a week in New York with her grandparents, my mother and Ron. She's only a little nervous about the flight, mostly excited; she's gone this route before, just not unaccompanied. In New York she'll see a Broadway show and visit the Bronx Zoo. Upstate where my parents have a butter-yellow farmhouse and thirty-odd acres, she'll read in the hammock, wade in the creek, ride horses every day.

I often flew alone as a kid. From the first grade until I was twelve, I lived in Massachusetts and my father lived in New Jersey, which meant I was shuttled back and forth for our occasional visits. Even so, I'm the one having trouble putting her on this plane. I remind her to lock the door when she uses the bathroom, and I confide that a man once caught me on the pot with my underpants around my ankles. For me it's like it happened yesterday. I still shudder when I remember that moment, intent on not being whooshed down the metal bowl before I managed to pull up my pants, straining to push the door shut with one foot, deeply absorbed in my Mary Janes all the way down the aisle and back to my seat, so as not to lock eyes with the oversized intruder, whoever he was.

Eliza smirks, embarrassed for me. "Mom," she says, "I'm not that dumb."

I watch her walk down the long corridor with accordion walls until she bears left onto the plane and I can't see her anymore. From a pay phone, I call my mother to tell her Eliza is on her way.

"I can't bear it," I whimper.

"Get used to it," my mother answers.

Another time, my mother asks me if I remember when my father abandoned me at the airport. I sputter in response. And then, "Just tell me," I say, playing for time.

She explains that I was flying alone, taking the Eastern shuttle from La Guardia, in Queens, to Logan, in Boston. "You were six, because I was pregnant with Andy," she remembers.

My mother and Ron had gone to the beach for the day with my brother Joe, who would have been turning two at the end of that summer. I was due home from New Jersey on the three o'clock shuttle.

"Your father decided to put you on an earlier flight. They had a party to attend in the afternoon."

She reminds me in those days there were no answering machines, no cell phones or pagers, no way to reach her, sitting with a book under a beach umbrella, all that white skin and thousands of freckles, while my brother and *his* father, my other father, searched for shells and made elaborate castles in the sand. When she got to the airport, my mother recalls, the personnel, the Eastern Airlines people, were really unglued.

"The first thing you said to me was that you had to go to the bathroom. You'd been afraid to go, afraid you'd miss me when I came to pick you up."

I'd waited three hours to pee.

It's peculiar to hear this story. I don't remember it, do I? And yet it's familiar, somehow, I have this visceral response: I feel the vinyl under my thighs, I smudge the chrome arm rests with the tips of my fingers, I tear at the scuffed patent leather at the heel of one of my shoes. I am squiggling in the sloping plastic chair to hold it in, squeezing my legs together, folding one into itself so that my heel presses against my crotch, waiting for my mother, who will come for me, I know.

"Just goes to show," my mother says, "how selective memory is," and I want to tell her I remember, because I *almost* do, but I don't.

Any actor worth her salt has dabbled in sense memory. Do I recall *specific* airport lighting (fluorescent), airport bathrooms (scuzzy), the red stripe along the back of my thigh from the airport chair, the pinch of the shiny strap and buckle across the top of my shoes, the space between my incisors, where only one of my two front teeth has begun to descend, the gum slick on one side and the edge of the tooth on the other slightly serrated? Are these generic memories, accumulated and resurrected at my convenience, at the slightest prompt, to serve whatever purpose I have in mind? Or are they real and specific to the event, and am I there again at La Guardia Airport, waiting for my mother?

And is my sudden sense of outrage for myself? Or am I angry at the thought that any child had to sit and wait with strangers for someone to take her home? Now that I have children of my own, children who tell me I'm overprotective, I'm shocked that my father prioritized the way he did. No doubt he told me to wait for my mother, she would come. No doubt he warned the flight attendants that my ride on the other end might be a tad delayed.

And with a start, I realize that I am unreasonably peeved with my mother and my stepfather for having gone to the beach without me. For being a family regardless of my absence. For having a life that continued in spite of the inconvenience of the first marriage, the odd child, who insinuated herself into every situation. And then I understand, not for the first time, how that sort of resentment goes both ways.

In any case, my mother recalls, I never flew alone again. From then on she accompanied me on the Eastern shuttle when I traveled to New York and amended the custody arrangements so that my father was compelled to do the same in the other direction.

"If it happened today," my mother says, "he'd be arrested for negligence."

Not long after his death, baffled by my grief and the shifts in our relationship, my mother told her psychiatrist the whole story. She says now that the doctor asked about my state of mind that day at the airport, my reaction when she finally arrived at the gate to take me home.

According to Leah, I was absolutely fine. I was her open book, the child who wore her proverbial heart on her sleeve. Nothing wrong with me that day other than the fact that I'd been holding my water for much too long.

The psychiatrist was impressed with what she determined was my sense of security and well-being. "She marveled at how much you must have trusted me," says my mother.

And I wonder, what makes us who we are? How is it that somebody is "fine" in the face of a scare at the age of six, and inexplicably miserable six months after the birth of her own daughter because she believes, right or wrong, that nobody ever felt about her the way she feels about this baby? How ridiculous is that?

There is a picture taken at Waukeela Camp for Girls in the summer of my thirteenth year. It's Parents' Weekend: we are standing in a grove of pine trees, my mother and I, her back to the camera; she is holding me in a tight embrace and my arms hang limp at my sides. Only my eyes appear over her shoulder (for by that time I am already almost 5' 5", nearly her height), and they are full to brimming with relief. This I do remember: my mother and Ron, driving up to New Hampshire from the new house, in Pelham, New York, were a few minutes late, the last of the parents to pull up the dirt road and park under the flagpole, tires crunching over pine needles. I'd been waiting and waiting, thinking they would never arrive.

Would I remember the airport episode if I had a photograph?

Why do I remember the time a man walked in on me in the lavatory—no photo, thanks very much—and not the time my father abandoned me in the airport? Could it have been that it wasn't so terrible being *abandoned*? *Abandoned* wasn't in my vocabulary. I had no idea that waiting for my mother for a few hours had such a terrifying label attached. But could it really have been that I wasn't one little bit worried or frightened?

Almost forty years later, who cares, what's the point?

The point is when my own children are waiting somewhere, I go pale and break out in a sweat if I'm running even five minutes late. (I admit I have issues about punctuality brought on, I believe, by Leah's theory—communicated early on—that tardiness is an indication of contempt; but that's another subject altogether.) The fact is, or so we're told, it's a different world today. Children, people, disappear all the time. Just check your milk cartons, your fliers from the postmaster general, your local news. Long before my own father came up missing, that's how I justified my anxiety.

And the other point? That shrink was right. I trusted my mother. I knew she would come. She was everything to me.

23 | Mythology

On a fall afternoon in 1962, my mother's younger sister, Abby, engaged to marry an Israeli with whom she would leave the country in a few years time, was baby-sitting for me and my brother Joe. In those days Leah wore her blue-black hair in a twist at the back of her head. Abby's, not quite so dark, was cut short to frame her face. Even so people mistook them for twins, the resemblance was that strong; high cheekboned, both, with short, straight noses, full lips, and shiny eyes. When Abby opened the door to the diaper service that afternoon (Joe wasn't even two years old), the man gaped at her.

"Mrs. Lenney, you've cut your hair," he exclaimed.

"No, no," Abby protested, "I'm not *me*, I'm my *sister!*"

A few years after my father's death, I call Noel on Christmas Day, as is customary, to wish her a happy birthday. Our occasional conversations have never been entirely fluent, although we both work hard at affability.

"And how is your sister?" she asks before we hang up.

"She's fine," I answer, astonished to think she remembers I have one. "She teaches school in Manhattan. Lives on the Upper East Side."

"She does?" Noel is obviously surprised. "But isn't she still married?"

"She's never been married."

"But," Noel protests, "but doesn't she have grown children, hasn't she been living in Israel all these years?"

I almost laughed. "That's my *mother's* sister," I tell her.

A pause before she titters, recovering herself, and then, "Yes, of course," she says, "that's who I meant, how is she, what's she doing these days?"

Is she embarrassed? Does she understand the implications of the exchange in the way that I do? No wonder she resented me so. A multitude of reasons for the tension between us, but to discover now, so long after the fact, that my father's second wife had never determined where Leah left off and I began.

And how can I fault her for that?

I'm not me, I might have explained at one time or another myself. *I'm my daughter.*

There was this thing that used to happen to me when I was a kid. Most times in the dark, when I was alone. I heard voices, one a grumble, a discontented growl, and the other a plea, high and plaintive. The voices rumpled the sheets. Soiled them. Bunched them up. Kept me from sleep. It didn't happen every night, just once in a while, but I'd have to turn on the lights and read to get rid of them. And then, one time, in the middle of the morning—I was taking a test in Mr. Simmons's eighth grade geometry, and I was ready to ace it—on came the voices. I couldn't think. I couldn't move my pencil. Broad daylight and the two of them were pummeling each other in my head. I focused on the pennies in my loafers until they blurred. The big, oblivious clock on the wall just ticked. I picked up my paper and pencil, slid out of my chair and walked up to the front of the room, my shoes slapping against the linoleum, halting for a moment the scratching of pencils—the occasional coughs, sneezes, and sighs—before my indifferent classmates went back to work.

"Mr. Simmons," I whispered to the top of his head behind his desk. He was bowed over a text, scalp all pink with a few fine, white hairs combed over the top. "Mr. Simmons, I need to be excused."

One look at me, he agreed. He wrote me a hall pass, I went to the office, and the nurse called my mother and told her, watching me all the time from the corner of her eye, "Your daughter says she's hearing voices." It never even occurred to me to fib.

My mother picked me up in the Ford Country Squire with the fake wood paneling.

"What kind of voices?" she wanted to know.

I explained that the voices were sad and angry. Not with me, I told her, with each other.

"All right, Dinah," said my mother. "The next time you hear those voices I want you to tell me, and I'm going to make them go away."

I never heard them again.

Recollection after recollection about fathers—fathers and daughters, fathers and sons—is characterized by searching and yearning to know the real guy. To pin him down. To figure him out. Whereas the mothers get the short end of the stick. The complaint. The gripe. The finger pointed in accusation. You ruined me, you ruined my life, you neglected me, you controlled me, you were overbearing, you weren't there enough, you never let me alone. It's all the mothers' fault, according to memoir. It's true: we blame our mothers for everything. And it's true we're justified in doing so. Because more often than not they were the primary caregivers making the decisions that mattered. Our fathers, however enlightened, however accessible, retained their mystery and their other lives, but our mothers? Our mothers were damned if they did and damned if they didn't. In our faces, or not, our mothers, who should have been omniscient and all-powerful if they weren't, will be blamed either way.

When Fred and I come home from a Sunday at the beach with the kids, we fall into predictable patterns of behavior: he unloads the car and disappears downstairs to his office, picks up his messages and his e-mail, opens a book, listens to some music, maybe returns a phone call, showers very possibly, invests in a little quiet for the sake of self-preservation. I'm in the kitchen unloading the coolers, rinsing the sand away, separating wet towels from suits, starting a load of wash, getting the kids in and out of the tub, putting on a pot of water for pasta, making sure this one has finished tomorrow's math and that one has given the saxophone a full twenty minutes. How strange it is to think that my own children will wonder about their father, as present as he is, will wonder at his secret life, his private person because he manages to hold on to himself and his time and space as separate and sacred. And it's inevitable they will blame me for one thing or another. Because I'm there to be blamed.

"Here we go," screams my mother, "here comes the mythology of Dinah's childhood! You've made this up, you're making this up!"

"I keep a file on you!" I shout back at her. "Do you know that? I keep a whole goddamn file!"

"I'll bet you do!"

It isn't true. I don't, I haven't, I only wish I had.

We're red-faced, shrieking at each other at the bottom of the spiral staircase in Echo Park. My children are asleep by now; my husband stands between us, my stepfather at the top of the stairs, interrupting intermittently with, "Leah, Leah, let's go, let's go now, Leah." I cannot remember how all this is resolved or even what it's about.

The mythology of my childhood: what I remember, what I've been told. What's true must lie somewhere in the middle, I suppose. Or is it altogether left or right of the respective fables?

Now when my own daughter sets her jaw, stares just past me, just over my shoulder, snaps, "All right, Mom," in that insolent little voice, I seethe with frustration. "Wipe that look off your face, or I'll wipe it off for you," Leah used to say, and more power to her, I'm thinking, confronted with Eliza's disdain. But my mother was barely out of her teens when I was born in the 1950s, whereas I have thirty-odd years on Eliza, and her father and I are well-educated in today's parenting philosophies. In spite of myself, I shout about what *my* mother would have done if I'd opened my mouth to her that way; I hurl invectives in Eliza's direction, culminating in some version of *who do you think you are anyway?* If this is as damaging as a slap in the face, no doubt someday she'll tell me so.

Back to my mother and me, though, circa 1971: there we were, straddling the table, on either side of the chandelier, faux bamboo with a monkey perched on one of the symmetrical branches. This is funny in retrospect: a teen-aged girl and her beautiful, young mother, playing an angry game of tag in the dining room, sliding on the wood floors in their winter socks, grabbing for purchase at the sideboard, digging deep into the oriental rug, screaming, until the mother somehow grabs the daughter by the hair and the daughter pulls away, stunned by the pain and the strands that come off in her fingers when she touches her scalp. She is taller than her mother and for the first time this makes a difference. They are face to face now and the mother, who is left-handed, pulls her arm back, open palm, thick gold band like a secret weapon on her ring finger, and the girl says, "So help me, Ma, if you hit me, I'm going to hit you back."

She never hit me again. In the spring of that year I got my period. I came home from an afternoon with friends at Split Rock, where I played Spin the Bottle for the first time, so nervous, so frightened to kiss a boy, worried I wouldn't know how. When the bottle pointed to me, John D., the cutest boy in the eighth grade, the one who would be boyfriend to a succession of best friends all the way through high school, said, "No way," got up off his haunches, and walked down the hill towards the cars. I was red in the face all the way home, hot to the tips of my ears, drowning in humiliation, until I saw the blood in my pants when I went to the bathroom and then, ecstatic, I rushed to the kitchen to tell my mother. She hugged me, she was thrilled, she wanted to tell my stepfather, who was weeding in the backyard, even after I told her no, please, no, and when I blocked her way out to the porch through the mud room, she fell back flat on her ass. She'd been foiled, and I was grounded for a week.

My stepfather protected my brothers and sister from my mother's wrath. I think he might have taken a belt to my brothers once or twice, but no one ever hit either of them in the face. It's subtle, this blood versus water thing—in a crisis, he left me to her—her standards for me were different, and he stayed out of her way. His remove served me and it didn't. Her single-minded focus served me and it didn't.

I was just a kid when my mother made me her confidante: she'd never loved my father, she'd wanted out before the wedding, and her mother had chided that the invitations were in the mail. Nelson was cruel, he ignored her, he punished her for cutting her hair, and he knocked the spoon from her hand when he thought she'd had enough to eat. When she miscarried a second child in the sixth month, a boy they would have called Adam, he wasn't even there. And when she fled to Miami to get her divorce, his mother, Rose, robbed her of her clothes and possessions, walked right in the front door and emptied her closets.

I loved to hear these stories. I loved to listen to my mother, to curl up beside her on her big bed, strewn with magazines and fabric swatches. I watched her paint her toes, read the paper, move the squares of color here and there; I was mesmerized by her hands, her freckled arms, her beautiful lips silently mouthing the clues to the crossword puzzle before she filled in the squares with her pencil. I loved the feel of the ironed sheets, and the smell of her skin, and I assaulted her with questions. How could she have refused to answer, relentless as I was even then?

"Did you ever think about going back to him, Mom? Was there ever a chance?"

She put down the newspaper and drew me close. "We were living in Miami, you and I," she said, "and your father flew down. He wanted to reconcile."

"Was I happy to see him?"

"Oh, honey, you were two, I suppose you were happy, you were a baby, you were always happy."

This made me laugh and I snuggled in closer.

"What was I like?"

"Oh, sweetie. You were wonderful. So easy, so much fun, everybody loved you."

More giggles. Very pleased with myself. Warm all over. If I could have crawled back inside her, I would have; the next best thing was to insinuate myself as her secret sharer, the one who really knew her, the one who really understood, the big little girl who was wise beyond her years.

"What happened? Tell me what happened."

"Grandpa Charlie called me," she said soberly. "He was opposed to the divorce, wanted us to patch it up, but he said there was something I should know before I made a decision . . ."

"What? What was it?"

Nelson had called my mother's father for a loan. When Charlie refused him, he asked if it'd be different if they weren't separated. Charlie equivocated, wouldn't commit either way. So Nelson flew down to Miami, took us to dinner, played with me, and pleaded with my mother to come home, to give it another try. He never mentioned the conversation with his father-in-law.

"So you see," said my mother, "I couldn't have gone back. Not once Grandpa told me the truth."

She was right, and I told her so, very solemn, very grown-up.

But this was a revelation. My father had tried to patch things between them. For cash! Money was always the issue, for as long as I could remember, they fought about money. Her child support was minimal and never increased, in spite of summer camp and orthodontics and inflation. How many times she tried to sue I cannot say, but no judge ever held him accountable. Leah claims she couldn't get an attorney worth his salt to take the case, reluctant, one and all, to alienate a politico, and convinced across the boards that my father was on a fast track to high elective office. So he wouldn't pay up, and he wouldn't disappear. If not for me, she could have forgotten him, there'd have been all sorts of possibilities, but with me in tow she had to look for another "daddy," and with me in tow she'd have contact with my father and his miserable family for the rest of her life.

The day after the sentencing, the day that picture of Noel and me appears in the *New York Times*, I meet my mother and her psychiatrist in Riverdale, a well-endowed, leafy community just north of the Bronx on the Metro North.

"I can't keep you on a pedestal," I tell her, both of us sitting in straight-backed chairs facing Gerda, a diminutive, old woman with a German accent. "I can't be your right arm anymore."

"Why not?" she sobs. "Why can't you?"

I roll my eyes at the doctor as if to say, *You see this? You see what I'm dealing with?*

"Mom," I say, "I'm married. I have a husband and two children. My life is about them."

"This," she informs Gerda through tears, "this was the central relationship of my life."

She is talking about me. She is talking about what she gave up to make things all right for me. She's wondering what might have happened the second time around, if she hadn't been looking for a husband *and* a father. This was a huge compromise for my mother, which is not to say she's filled with regret. How can she be? She bore three more children, carved herself a career out of nothing, served a family and a community, and remains married to my stepfather over forty years later. So much to show for her efforts, so many things to be proud about.

"Do you have any regrets?" Eliza asks me one day.

"We all have regrets," I say.

"But you're glad you married Daddy? You're glad you have us?"

When you look at the children, *your* children, regrets evaporate. If you'd done anything differently, they wouldn't exist. If those children are the sum of your choices and experience, how can you possibly wish it had gone any other way?

My mother cannot regret her relationship with my father, I reason, since otherwise she wouldn't have me. Even so, anyone can see she's full of rage. When she allows herself to consider, she's furious and confused by my ingratitude. She took care of me to the best of her ability, didn't she? Didn't she make me the *central relationship of her life?*

"I didn't kill your father, Dinah!" Her voice trembles.

"Of course you didn't," I answer. "I know you didn't."

"I protected you," she shouts across the room. "I protected you from him!"

And I did my part, too. Anxious to please and determined to survive, I accepted that she'd been wronged, and I figured out how to take care of her. I stroked her, coddled her, made sure she knew I loved her best. I believed her, too. Believed that my father was mean. Difficult. Shallow. Unscrupulous. Incapable of emotion. Incapable of love. I commiserated to ensure her devotion and my security. I didn't want her to know how I adored my father, identified with him, because I didn't want to risk her disappointment, and even worse, her disapproval. I needed her.

Years later I understood what my mother meant by *protect.* It wasn't a matter of custody, of physical proximity. In those days, no child from a "broken home" spent all that much time with her father unless the father was particularly attentive and available, which mine was not. No, my mother believed she'd protected me with insight, with the truth, as she saw it, about my father's character.

My brother Joe is divorced and shares custody and support of his children with his ex-wife. My parents, sad as they are about the failed marriage, are proud of the way Joe and Ellen are bringing up their kids. Everyone knows, nowadays, that a parent must never undermine the other parent in front of the children. You don't bad-mouth the ex. You don't enlist the kids on your behalf. You don't ask them to take sides.

Back then divorced parents weren't so enlightened. My mother was determined that I know, even as a small child and for my own good, that my father was a bad guy. In this way she would *protect* me from outsized fantasies and overwhelming disappointment. How frustrating for her that I fantasized anyway. And how could she have known the extent of my imaginings? I absorbed, and nodded, and empathized. But bad guy or not, I curled up under the sheets in the dark and told myself elaborate stories that involved Composite Man—my own superhero—nearly equal parts my father and my stepfather. He was tall like Nelson, bespectacled like Ron, athletic like Nelson, and he made the best scrambled eggs like Ron. In my fantasies I overwhelmed my complicated circumstances with a better story. I made myself a composite, too, smaller, more delicate, and the favorite child without a doubt. Confused in spite of my mother's best efforts, it pained me to be the sole and constant reminder of the biggest mistake of her life. I wondered, naturally, about heredity in all its aspects and implications. I tried so hard to be a good girl. I tried so hard not to be Nelson's daughter in any obvious ways, to keep her and my stepfather from making the association, to assure her I'd turn out okay in spite of that half of my gene pool. Still, some small stubborn part of me wasn't buying it, didn't want to believe her; all the evidence in the world couldn't convince me entirely. I wasn't, I still am not so sure he was such a terrible person. Flawed, yes. But evil?

These days my mother and I are certain, both of us, she never should have told me the things she did. The truth is relative at best and not always worth sharing. But my mother thought she was *protecting* me. It never once occurred to her it was the other way around. Not even when I stopped doing my part. Not even when I left her to flounder without my support and encouragement and *protection*, did she understand fully what she'd lost.

24 | Two Fathers

Eliza was induced two weeks after her due date, and late the following afternoon my doctor performed an emergency C-section while Ron and Leah waited in the reception area of the maternity ward at Cedars-Sinai Medical Center. When they wheeled me out of surgery, my parents were standing in the corridor; Leah rushed to me, her own baby, to make sure I was all of a piece, and Ron rushed to Eliza, cradled in Fred's arms, to count her fingers and toes.

The next time, with Jake, I insisted on having a vaginal birth, in spite of the odds. Again my parents were on the West Coast, but my mother was in San Francisco when I went into labor, and it was Ron who first met his grandson, who stood in line to hold the baby right after Fred and me.

Nelson came to LA to meet his granddaughter for the first time, when she was four months old. Together we gazed over the top rail of the crib, where she alternately cooed and shrieked, reaching for the mobile above her, struggling to turn herself over, flirting, teasing, ogling me until I reached in to pick her up, and then she pressed herself to me and gave him a big, sloppy smile as if to say, *This one here, this is mine.*

"Christ, she's so happy," said my father, reaching out to take her, then holding her high against his chest in the crook of his elbow.

"Doesn't she move you?" I asked him.

"You move me," he said.

The story goes that my mother dated like mad in the aftermath of the divorce. She was twenty-three years old; smart, accomplished, absolutely gorgeous. Suitor after suitor would tell her to get a sitter and off they'd go to dinner, to the opera, to a movie, for a weekend in the country; then along came Ron Lenney, who'd grown up in the Bronx, who said "chawcolate," who hadn't attended the Ivy League, who'd put himself through night school to get his law degree, who loved kids, all shapes, all sizes. He'd say something along the lines of, *Let's pack a picnic, and we'll take Dinah to the beach*, and she knew she'd found the right guy.

I called him *Dad* from the start, and I used his last name, with Nelson's permission, all through elementary school, although Ron only legally changed it for me around my sixteenth birthday, just before I acquired a driver's license. It seems peculiar now that Nelson ever acquiesced to such a thing, but I wanted so badly to be a member of a real family, besides which, prepubescent kids are notoriously cruel. Every September from kindergarten on, my teachers, no fault of theirs, were bound to call me by my name as it appeared in the attendance records until my mother set them straight. Every year class clown Eddie Miller, skinny with greasy hair and buckteeth, jeered on cue across the room: "Dinah *Gross*, ha, ha, *gross, gross*, you're *gross*." At some point Nelson relented and I prevailed; *Dinah Gross* disappeared altogether by the time I was ten. *Dinah Lenney* it was.

As for Ron, my mother gives me credit for winning him over, for bringing him round. By the time I was twelve or so, she used to say, it was as though I was his own child. How come I never quite bought it? Now with children of my own and the consequential heartache and responsibility, I don't know how he managed it, or how to thank him either. Ron has never been one for protracted analysis or discussion; in the middle of the argument about the mythology of my childhood, he simply states, "We do not remember things as you do. But if that's your recollection, we should talk about it sometime."

"Remember," he said to me not long ago, "how you and I used to walk together on the beach, that winter we lived in Hull?"

"Yes," I nod, even though I don't, still eager to please, still unable to trust that forty years of proximity will establish a rapport that will compensate for our genetic differences. It's almost enough for me that my daughter has won this man's heart, although I'm vaguely, irrationally hurt when he tells me, in passing, how different she is from me. Is that why she's lovable? My stepfather—vigilant, consistent, tolerant, benevolent—loved me, I assumed, *in spite* of who I was.

Before my father died I never used the word *step*. I avoided *step* like crazy; it didn't fit, it had nasty connotations, and it didn't work with my strategy; that is, if I pretended hard enough it was real, it would be real between us.

I still flush inwardly with pleasure when he introduces me as his daughter. I love knowing that he carries photographs of my children in his wallet. I'm proud beyond the pale when he takes my side, expresses indignation on my behalf, sympathy for my plight. And when he tells me I've done something well? When he says he's always known I was capable of making the right choice? First I'm delighted with both of us, and then I wonder at the tacit implication; I was capable of the wrong choice also, wasn't I? I take his commitment for granted but not his love.

As for demonstrated affection, it isn't far-fetched to claim to be able to count on my fingers the number of times he's hugged me. Everyone knows the Lenneys are not touchy-feely types, not big on public displays of any kind. There's a story his mother used to tell about Ron as a boy. They got on a train to visit his own grandmother, and he cried all the way there. His mother mostly ignored him until she couldn't stand it anymore. Finally she asked him, exasperated, why he was crying. "It's Gramma," he sobbed. "She kisses so wet."

My stepfather's family was a close-knit clan, devoted to each other and deliberately unsentimental. I think I must have spent a fair amount of my childhood holding his hand and sitting in his lap. But like all eldest children, not just quasi-adopted ones, I was usurped by the next one and the next one and the next one down. He called me *Babe*—still does—and he rubbed my neck and shoulders with his strong, square-tipped fingers straight through my high school exams, but sometime in my late teens he established a careful physical boundary between us. It made perfect sense that he cuddled with Jill, almost thirteen years younger than I. Not so easy, though, to understand why he'd greet one of my friends with a kiss on the cheek or a quick squeeze and keep me at arm's length. When I left for Europe in the winter of my senior year of high school to be a foreign exchange student, we shook hands in good-bye. I'd reached out as a joke, thinking he'd pull me to him for a hug. "So long, Babe," he said, shaking with one hand, patting my shoulder with the other. Apparently my mother, in tears, excoriated him all the way home.

Nor was Nelson openly affectionate. His kisses were perfunctory and he wrangled out of any embrace as quickly as he could. It's too simple, and a little paranoiac, I guess, to chalk all this up to genetic material, but that's what I did. Ron didn't want to get too close to me because I'm too much like Nelson.

Nelson didn't want to get too close because I'm too much like Leah. Whatever it was, I was bound to over-think it.

The other day I called Ron from the car to tell him he was a wonderful father. I could hear the smile in his voice.

"Are you watching the road?" he asked.

"I am," I said.

"Are you overcome with emotion?"

"As a matter of fact, I am," I answered.

"All right, then," he said. "Thanks for the call, Babe."

Not that I don't think my siblings have ever told him so, but the thing is, they don't have to. They take Ron and unconditional love for granted: of course, he's a good father, that's his job. I should know by now, words and demonstrations—from Ron, that is—aren't forthcoming or necessary. It is what it is, that's all. Except that I owe him big time. And if you're going to take on somebody else's kid, she ought to let you know every now and then that she's grateful.

In any case I wooed them both, my father and my stepfather. Oh yes, they were stuck with me, but I was relentless, determined—insatiable, I suppose—but ultimately winning. Neither one of them chose the path of least resistance. Neither one of them ever let go. And in the end, I must believe, their devotion to my children has to be evidence of their great affection for me.

25 | My Father under My Fingernails

In Autumn of 1999, we're adopted by a white pigeon. I'm making the bed one morning when I notice him perched on the railing of the deck outside. All white with a damaged wing, caked with dirt and dried blood, this is perhaps why he moves not at all as I approach the sliding glass door to look more closely. For several days he hops from the railing to a branch on the Chinese elm and back to the railing, the bad wing fluttering awkwardly at his side. He's there when we open our eyes at dawn, and late in the night he glows in the dark, a fallen star of a bird, alert and watchful before we fall asleep to his throaty crooning.

I can't decide whether I'm annoyed or flattered. On the one hand the deck is covered with pigeon poop; on the other, he is ghostly and rare, dignified in spite of his wounds and the mess he's making. It appears we've been chosen, and much as I'd like him to move on, I don't wish to offend him.

"His name is Maurice," Jake says one morning, with supreme confidence.

"Maurice?" queries Fred. "How do you know?"

"I just know," Jake says.

"Maurice," mutters Fred. "Where the hell did he come up with a name like that?"

A friend, a vegetarian, who feeds her three dogs and two cats barbecue from her own hands and lets them lick her fingers, suggests that we give Maurice something to eat.

"Oh no, you don't," says Fred. "Don't you dare feed that bird, we'll never get rid of him."

And then one day, the pigeon glides on both wings from the Chinese elm all the way to the top of the eucalyptus in the far corner of the backyard. I'm thrilled that he's well enough to fly and afraid I'll never see him again.

Thankfully he's back the next morning, watching me pull up the spread and plump the pillows from his spot on the railing.

I tiptoe to the sliding screen door and stare out at him, an arm's length away, eyes darting but unafraid, entirely at ease. His wing is nearly healed, just a shadow of the wound is visible. Nobody's home, but even so I look around me to make certain, so as not to get caught, so as not to be publicly humiliated, before I whisper, "Dad?"

But now he's not even looking at me. I chuckle aloud to cover my embarrassment. I even blush. I'm ridiculous, I know.

Two more days the bird spends on our decks, in our trees, and then, on the third, I catch sight of him on the tiled roof of a house in the valley below, just before he spreads his wings and sails away forever.

It takes me a full year to do something about the ashes. They sit on a shelf in the closet just in front of a stack of winter sweaters and jeans that don't fit. I'd tried just once to open the box, realized it was sealed shut and abandoned it there, stopping every now and then to give it a shake (it rattles— my God, are those bones?), knowing that if I were to force it open it would spill onto the carpet to be vacuumed away, and somehow I don't want the smallest particle of my father to be whooshed up into the Oreck with dog hair and cookie crumbs and toenail clippings. He sits unopened on the lowest shelf of the closet because I cannot decide where this third of him belongs. In the mountains (don't go there much)? In the garden (what if we move?)? In the park (to be dug up by a stray dog)? Would he even want to be in California? Was this unfair, to bring one third of my father so far west?

In the end I decide it's only unjust that he sits on a shelf in the dark encased in painted cardboard, domed and carved like a treasure chest but nothing more than a file box, really. He needs to be freed, released to the elements, to swirl away in wind and water, become part of the sand, part of the sea, ashes to ashes.

The kids are not invited. Over a year ago we threw roses into Echo Park Lake in Pop's honor, which would have made him laugh, I hope. Just irreverent enough, the idea of waterlogged flowers floating around in that polluted pond with snapping turtles, candy wrappers, used condoms, and toxic fish, nudged aside by aggressive ducks looking for crumbs, passed by a couple of snooty urban swans who couldn't be bothered. And on the first anniversary of his death, we lit a yarzheit candle as Jews are supposed to, remembered him with stories and impersonations. Somehow, though, I don't think my children are ready to know that matter equals matter, that their grandfather has been reduced to a box full of soot. Do I underestimate them, or is it that I cannot bear to share? All I know is I want to do this quietly, without explaining, selfishly, without making the ritual meaningful for anyone else.

Fred and I drive out to Point Dume on Saturday, January 9, 1999, a year and some months after my father's death, the day he would have turned sixty-seven. It's a jewel of a morning, there's a strong breeze, and we walk toward the surf and then trudge south against the wind, squinting into the sun, pass a few sunbathers, a family with a toddler, a couple of guys sitting on surfboards, until we are just in front of a huge boulder about three hundred yards off shore. A landmark, a way to remember the general idea of the place.

Fred pries open the box with the Swiss Army knife on his key ring. The contents are darker than I thought, and heavier, not white and feathery like ashes in the fireplace, but gray, almost black, and they sort of stick to my fingers.

"On the outgoing," whispers my unobtrusive husband, not wanting the stuff to fly back in my face when I drop it into the waves. We alternate, each with a handful, until we reach the bottom, the pebbly pieces, the bones that rattled are the last of him, and we let them go with the rest.

"Boo," shouts a man just behind us, and I jump. He guffaws, and says, "Oh very serious," and walks on without looking back, and I want to shout back at him, *Yes, damn right we're serious, this is my father, these are his ashes, he was murdered less than two years ago, you asshole.* I'm trembling, half-laughing, half-crying, and Fred points out to where just beyond the big rock, a dolphin leaps in and out of the waves on its way out to sea.

"There he goes," says Fred.

We chuck the empty gold box in a trash can before we reach the car. Even now I can't help wishing I'd kept one pebble, one piece for my pocket, for the night table drawer, the jewelry tin, the safe deposit box, for under my pillow, for between the socks, for what? For *what*?

My mother fully intended to make a necklace of all our baby teeth, but who would ever wear such a thing? Now she uses the teeth to prove to unsuspecting children that their parents are big liars.

"Look, Eliza," she told my daughter the summer she was six and had lost a tooth, another hanging by a shred from her upper gum. "There's no such thing as the tooth fairy, see? I have all your mommy's baby teeth in a box upstairs. I'll show you after breakfast." Then, as she finished her coffee, "I don't believe in lying to children, all that nonsense, all that gobble-dygook, it's ludicrous," she said.

Evidence. She kept the evidence, and but for the gray line under the rim of my index finger, I have thrown all my evidence to the sea.

26 | Resentment

Until after I was married I never saw a picture of myself on display in any of my father's houses. There were a couple of pages of baby Polaroids in a monogrammed album in the bookshelves in the guest room. And my father had a few shots of me tacked to a fabric board on the top shelf of his closet, behind his watch and his cufflinks. But nothing for public consumption. Noel arranged her silver-framed photos, all shapes and sizes and most of them black and white, on a round damask-covered table in the living room; images of her and my father, of course, together and with Neil, with governors, with senators, with presidents, too.

Then, the first time Fred and I visited Dark Horse Farm in Bridgehampton, one of our wedding photos mysteriously appeared the morning after we arrived, stuffed into a Lucite frame a half an inch too small on every side, and perched precariously on top of the big-screen TV with its massive, sloped exterior.

Once the kids were born, I was happy and proud to send my father pictures every few months or so, with no thought to whether he showed them off or he didn't. After his death the photographs come back to me, packed inside a box of shirts (I'd asked for them), clean and starched, and even so they smell of his cologne, of him; I want to wear them like smocks, untucked, with the sleeves rolled to the elbow, except I'm loathe to launder them and wash that smell away.

But the pictures! First I wonder where he kept them all those years; then I'm glad to know he kept them at all, and glad to have them back.

For a month or so after the murder I speak to Aunt Gayle once a week. She checks in with me on Fridays. She's tough but loyal, unsentimental but consistently generous, determined, as she was when I was a little girl, to keep me in the family loop. And I'm thankful.

Less than a week after the memorial service, Paul calls to talk to us both, Fred and me, about writing my father's story. We mull the idea for a day or two before we beg off. It's too soon to dive headfirst into the emotional swamp from which I haven't yet emerged. Paul says he understands; he intends to write the book anyway, with or without us. When Gayle mentions several weeks later that he's finished a draft, I'm astounded. Apparently it's been sent out to agents and editors. "Nobody wants anything to do with it," she adds as an afterthought.

It all goes bad between Paul and me when I do as he counsels, hire a lawyer to represent my interests in my father's estate. Not that I hadn't already considered doing so once it was discovered that my father had botched his will—"fucked it all up" in my stepmother's words—but I'm relieved to have Paul think it's his idea. Unfortunately he doesn't like the guy I choose, that is, the guy my mother and Ron choose for me. My lawyer meanders, and his style, fussy and a little vague, irritates Paul, who wants to move quickly.

"Trust me," my uncle says, weeks into the ordeal. "Let's get past this now, let's try to move on."

I remind him he insisted I hire somebody. I ask what he wants of me.

"I want to honor my brother's intentions, that's all."

He urges me to let *him* take care of everything. As if I could. As if I had any choice in the matter. The will is a disaster; we're all in way over our heads.

"He isn't Solomon!" I tell Gayle, who believes I'm disloyal.

"Yes, he is!" she cries.

"You have betrayed us!" she accuses.

"I can never be close to you again!" she threatens.

Paul wants to honor my father's intentions. So he cuts me off. He stops speaking to me. He sends me carefully dictated letters about legal matters, taxes, binding agreements, insurance policies, and after my grandfather's death (my having inherited half my father's portion of the estate), back taxes due.

In the months just after the murder, I long to be close to my father's brothers, and I yearn for them to recognize him in my children. Smarting from their disapproval, wounded by their consequent indifference, I'm reminded that my father dismissed his family entirely but for the occasional business deal. They rarely socialized, and the women, at least, bad-mouthed each other every chance they got. Suddenly I'm the pariah, the scapegoat, the money-grubber. *Well, if that serves to make them feel like a family, I tell myself, let them have each other; I didn't need them before, and I sure as hell don't need them now.*

If shared sorrow is easier to bear, I wouldn't know. As Gayle and Paul grow cool and distant, just before we stop speaking altogether, I'm tangled up in a grief that won't quit. Please, I want to say, please, don't write me off, I'm his daughter, I'm your niece, help me, won't you help me, please?

As for Noel, we try on the phone a couple of times in the first few months and oh, the strain of it.

"You have a life," she laments, "but what will become of me?"

The pretense is short-lived. The stab at closeness too little, too late, too contrived. My stepmother and I were never friends. My half-brother Neil has always been a stranger. My father, our only connection, is dead.

27 | Conjecture

As the parents of a toddler, Christmas, 1991, we brought along the camcorder. Fred videotaped the occasion, but as it turned out, I never got out of the way long enough for the camera to linger on my father.

I can hear his voice in my head. I can picture him in a chair, slouched, chewing his thumb, legs spread wide. But I can't get him walking and talking at the same time. My father exists for me in snatches, in fragments—in a flash of recognition, a remembered phrase, a snapped still—and always as my father, not in any other guise. It jolts me to realize how little I knew of his *real* life. I didn't think to ask questions, to take note; I was so busy trying to get his attention, it never occurred to me to pay attention myself. So I long for dreams, for stories, for access and answers. I want so badly to understand what happened to him, to make sense of it.

Focus on the living, said my mother. *There's so much to live for.*

Let's get past this now, said my uncle. *Let's try to move on.*

Yes, of course. But when we find that tape from Christmas 1991, six months after his death, I can't get close enough to the television. I can't believe he's there—alive!—talking to my baby, offering her a cracker. I can't believe I keep crossing in front of him, preempting, directing, orchestrating, controlling.

And if I'd gotten out of the way? What then? What secret might have been revealed? Easier for a stranger to accept these events, if not to comprehend them. Easier to imagine a stranger, so that's what I do, knowing what I know and in spite of what I don't, I can't help but wonder and obsess.

The man, alone in his office, telephone wedged between his ear and his shoulder, tells his wife he will meet her at the appointed time and place. "All right, Noel. I said I would. I'll be there. All right."

He hangs up the phone. Behind him, from the rear window of the bungalow, beyond the fake paneling and the freckled walls, he can see his boat, a huge, white ferry, streamers flying, flags at full mast. There's a bread truck at the bottom of the ramp, and the smell of fish wafts in from the parking lot, mostly empty, it's only nine o'clock, after all, a warm day for the middle of September, the day manager doesn't even start picking up lunch reservations until after ten.

A chef, in a white double-breasted jacket and checkered pants, trudges up the ramp and through the double doors, polished mahogany and brass fittings, stopping just before he enters to remove a wad of gum from his shoe, tossing it over the guard ropes, thick and twisted, into the murky harbor below.

The man chews the cuticle on the side of his thumbnail and watches the restaurant wake up until he hears the door click closed behind him. He swivels back around in his chair to see a young man, a boy really, brown-skinned and slight, wearing a dark knit cap, pointing a revolver at his chest with both hands.

"Don't do nothing stupid, Mr. Gross," says the boy.

The man remembers this face from somewhere, pouting, small-featured, turned-up nose like a woman's. Who the hell . . .? Oh, Jesus, it's that busboy, Christian—Christian something—he'd been fired a while back, showed up late or not at all for a couple of shifts, Jesus, who needed it, plenty just like him where he came from, he'd been working on the boat off and on for a year and he knew the rules, no more excuses, no more breaks.

Leaning back in his chair, the man asks, "What are you doing here? What do you want?"

"Hey, I said, don't move! Don't do nothing, just sit there till I tell you, mister, you see this gun, you see it?"

"Okay, okay, calm down," says the man, with his hands up. Then he crosses his arms over his chest. "What do you want?"

"You got to give me a hundred thousand dollars," says Christian. And maybe one of his eyes is twitching, imperceptible, the boy would like to rub at the spasm with his forefinger, but instead he grips the gun harder and raises it a little.

The man shakes his head and snorts. "Don't be stupid," he says.

"Hey, Mr. Gross, you think this is funny? I'll fucking shoot you," says Christian. "I'll do it, I swear."

"Look," says the man, "I don't have that kind of money to give you. I'm not liquid like that. You think I keep that kind of cash in the bottom drawer here?"

He rolls closer to the desk to open it and the boy barks, "I said don't move!" The gun wobbles and jerks in his grip. "I know you're rich, old man."

"No one keeps money like that around," the man says, wiping his nose with the back of his hand.

"Get up real slow, Mr. Gross. Get up and walk out of here and bring those," says Christian, gesturing with the gun to the silver ring of keys between the phone and an old-fashioned Rolodex.

Outside, the smell of river mud and autumn on the way, the man buttons his linen blazer and looks toward the ferry, where a couple of workers heave boxes from the bread truck onto a dolly. It's just after nine and Marge, the manager, won't be in for an hour.

"You're driving, Mr. Gross," whispers Christian from just behind him. "Unlock your big car."

An old brown Mazda is idling next to the man's BMW, parked between spaces just outside the bungalow. Another boy, small like Christian but with curly hair, jumps off the hood as the man comes around to the driver's side of his sedan.

"Hurry up," says Christian, still pointing the gun from inside his wind breaker, rubbing furiously at the offending muscle just above his eyelid with his other hand.

"It's open," says the man as he lowers himself into the driver's seat. Christian leans in the window of the Mazda to talk to the driver, then gets in the BMW on the passenger side. The other kid, the one who was sitting on the hood, climbs in back.

"Take us to the bank, mister. Take us to the Bank of New York.

"My bank is right there," says the man, pointing to a branch on the other side of the parking lot.

"No way, man, not here. We're going to the city."

The man sighs hard through his nose. "I can't get you cash in New York," he says.

"Just drive," says Christian. "Don't do nothing funny 'cause I'll shoot you dead, I swear."

Now as the man pulls his car out of the lot and heads up River Road, the Mazda right behind him, maybe now he thinks to himself that these are just kids, a couple of kids playing games for Christ's sake. "Where are we going?" he asks coasting to a stop at a yellow light.

"Take the bridge, I'll tell you where to go."

Winding up the narrow curve toward the top of the hill, the man sees a dark-green Jeep Cherokee coming the other way; his son, Neil, on his way into the restaurant where he is next in the chain of command and works full time. Neil waves and the man waves back without making eye contact, but he sees his son searching in the rearview mirror, turning his head, trying to figure out who his father has in the car. If Neil swerves just a little in his preoccupation, the man thinks to himself, Damn it, watch the road, will you? Don't you know how to drive?

The car phone starts to ring.

"Don't pick it up," says Christian.

It keeps ringing.

The guy in the backseat says something to Christian in Spanish.

The phone stops ringing. Starts again.

"Shit," says Christian.

"It's my son," says the man. "It's Neil," he says again.

"Well, tell him—tell him something," Christian orders.

"What are you doing?" asks Neil, when his father picks up the phone.

"It's just business," says the man. "I'll see you later," he adds, and he hangs up.

Could be now the busboy implicates the man's son. Maybe he suggests that Neil owes somebody money for something. Maybe this is why the man doesn't drive straight to the police station in Edgewater, never mind the gun in the back of his head.

If this is so, the man looks hard at Christian as he slows for the tollbooth.

"Listen," he says, "you leave Neil alone. You don't deal with my son. Ever. Just deal with me, I'll take care of you."

The kid in the backseat leans forward. "We want a hundred thousand bucks."

"Forget it," says the man, "I told you, I don't have it, I'll give you twenty."

The boys speak to each other in Spanish as they exit the highway in Washington Heights, in caravan with the Mazda, and drive to the neighborhood branch of the Bank of New York. Their voices are high and soft, and Christian's hand on the gun is small like a child's. The man must be thinking that the gun is a problem, that otherwise it'd be easy enough to teach this punk a lesson.

Inside the bank, before he steps toward the teller, Christian warns low in his ear, "Don't try nothing, mister, I'm watching you."

Back in the car, the man turns his key in the ignition and asks, "Where now?"

"You said you'd give us twenty," says Christian, almost whining.

"Don't be a dummy," says the man. "You live in America now. I told you, I have to get it at my own branch. I can't just walk into any bank and ask for twenty grand in cash. It doesn't work like that."

"Can you get it back at the boat?"

"I told you I could."

"Then drive, Mr. Gross. And don't try nothing stupid."

The man drives back over the George Washington Bridge to New Jersey, the brown Mazda several cars back, weaving in and out of the traffic to catch up.

Back at the branch across the parking lot from the restaurant, the man fills out a withdrawal slip and hands it to the teller. Christian leans against the wall holding the sports section of the Daily News. The other two boys wait outside in the Mazda, with the motor running, parked just behind the silver BMW.

The man is talking too long to the woman behind the glass, so Christian closes the paper and walks up behind him. The teller is smiling. Maybe she has a bad permanent and lipstick on one of her two front teeth. The man smiles back at her, before turning to Christian.

"How do you want it?" he asks. "Big bills?"

"That's good," says Christian, his voice cracking a little.

Outside the bank he tells the man, "Okay Mr. Gross, get back in the car."

"Hey. No," the man says, shoving his hands in his blazer pockets. "We made a deal, you got your money. Get out of here now—get going and let me go back to work."

Christian says something in Spanish to his friend, still in the back of the BMW, keeping the gun in his jacket pocket trained on the man. Maybe he is quiet for a moment, measuring, calculating; the man, in a navy blue jacket, creased pants, and a leather belt, is over six feet tall, must weigh more than two hundred pounds.

"No way, Mr. Gross," he hisses, "I can't leave you here. You could call the cops. You got to come with us—get in the car, get in, and we'll let you go later."

It's now, perhaps, that the boy's last name comes to the man, unasked for, unbidden, rises up in the front of his eyes now as clear as the bold print on his paycheck. "Hey, wait a minute, Velez, that wasn't our deal," says the man.

Does the boy wince at the sound of his own last name? Does his eye begin to twitch again?

"Get in and drive, Mr. Gross. I ain't telling you again."

The lot, as big as a football field, is still mostly empty. It's only 11:00 and the Ferry doesn't serve lunch before 11:30. The theaters have opened their doors but only a few moments before. Maybe a woman in a suit and sensible pumps is getting out of her car, heading into the bank, shuffling through her bag, almost brushing elbows with the man as she reaches the heavy glass doors.

"Excuse me," she says without looking up, triumphantly pulling her wallet from the bottom of her purse and pushing her way inside.

The man gets into the car and drives one more time out of the ferryboat parking lot. Again, he weaves his way up River Road, over the bridge and onto the West Side highway. He would be angry now, distracted; his wife is waiting for him in a store on Madison Avenue where they're supposed to choose knobs for the new kitchen cabinets. He stares out the window, drives with one hand, chews the cuticle on his other thumb, pays no attention to the other two men in the car, who blabber away in a foreign language, for Christ's sake, abusing their privileges as residents of America. Maybe it occurs to him as he slows for the toll, to drive into the tollbooth, to come to a stop, throw the keys out the window, less damage, less hassle; but he doesn't want to create a scene, a traffic jam, he can handle the situation, it's annoying, damned inconvenient, and he'll make these punks pay, he will, but for now, for now, he tells himself, he'll just do what they want and get the ordeal over with.

They are cruising along the West Side Highway, when the man asks them again where the hell they are going.

Abruptly, Christian tells him to pull over to the side of the road, to park beside the guardrail in the breakdown lane.

"Christ," mutters the man.

"Just pull over, Mr. Gross. Do it now!" orders Christian, with the nose of the gun pressed into the man's neck, and the man does what he asks, wanting to push the gun away, forcing himself to keep both hands on the steering wheel.

"Now what?" he says putting the car in park.

"Get out," says the kid.

The man sees the Mazda pull up behind his own big gray car.

"Get out," the kid tells him again.

"Look," says the man, "I don't want to get out. Let me go now. You've got what you want. Let me go."

"I told you get out of the car." The gun is cold against his neck and the man opens the driver door.

He gets out, straightens his blazer, walks to the passenger side of the car with both hands clenched in his pockets. He is sweating in the September sun. Christian stands behind him, holding his arm with the gun in his back. The other two are over by the Mazda, gesturing, arguing in Spanish. Foreigners, the man must be thinking, little, dark men, a couple of sissies shrieking at each other like girls, waving their small hands in each other's faces, wasting his time. One of them throws up his arms, shakes his head. Gets back in the brown car but makes no move to drive away. Leans back in the seat, licks his lips and closes his eyes.

The other one comes up beside the man.

"Come on," he says.

"Where?" says the man. "Where am I supposed to go?"

The kid grabs his elbow and steps over the cement guardrail.

"Climb over," he orders. "You go first, down there, to the river."

"Come on," the man scoffs. "We can't walk down there. There's no path. It's too steep."

"Move," says the kid.

The man steps over the rail easily and looks down to the Hudson. It's a steep incline, nearly vertical, thick with shrubs, tall grass, ivy and brambles, wooded with skinny birch and elm trees. The traffic screams by but no one stops, no one wonders at the tall, gray-haired businessman and his two young Latino companions. No one registers the big BMW and the beat-up brown Mazda parked in tandem. The midmorning light filters through the trees and the water glints in the sun some five hundred yards below. The man takes a step in his flat, black loafers, slides, catches himself before he goes all the way down, grabs a fist full of bush, winces, and pulls himself up.

"Jesus, there's no path," he mutters, but the gun is in his back, and he steps down again through the tangled brush and trips. His knee buckles and twists under his own weight. It's bad, he knows it; if he doesn't ice it soon, it'll be trouble.

By the time they reach bottom, he's ripped his jacket sleeve, and the palms of his hands are stinging, splintered and torn from brambles and thorny weeds along the slope where he's grabbed for purchase, to keep from sliding all the way. His knee is starting to swell, along with one elbow, and his khakis are grass-stained and damp at the seat, from sliding and falling several feet in spite of his efforts.

"Now what?" he asks, taking off his jacket, wiping the dirt and perspiration from his brow.

"Sit," says the kid.

"Why?"

"We just want to talk to you," says the one whose name he doesn't know.

"What are you going to do? Tie me up and leave me here?"

"I told you sit!" the kid screams.

It's quiet down here by the river; the traffic is only a hum, a vibration. A squirrel chitters and scolds from above and a mourning dove sings back at him. To the north a sailboat courses the river, and the man can see his Ferry, filling now with people for an early lunch. They should do at least a hundred covers before two, since the day is fine, mild for fall. God, it's warm, the man thinks, as he sits on a boulder, glancing for a moment at the incline behind him. A fucking 90 degree angle, for chrissakes, how the hell am I going to get back up there? Maybe he massages the bad knee with the bruised heel of his palm. Maybe he undoes the second button on his shirt, ignoring his abductors, who are standing in the brush behind him, whispering in a language he doesn't care to understand.

Suddenly, a shock of pain to the back of his head. His vision goes black for an instant, he struggles to right himself, feels a trickle behind his ear, reaches up to touch it, thick, warm like syrup, Jesus Christ, it's blood, it's his blood, he's bleeding from the back of his head, from a blow, the dropping of a rock, and now one of the boys faces him, throwing stones from just a few feet away. He raises his hands to shield his face, his forehead. What's going on? They were supposed to tie him up and leave him here, what the hell is going on?

He's down now, he's fallen to the ground, he's trying to pull his body up when he sees Christian coming toward him, something in his hand, not the gun, where's the gun, the gun is nowhere to be seen. Christian wields a knife instead, a pocketknife, and he thrusts it at the man who cannot get to his feet, who can only raise his hands again, falling backward, crossing his arms in front of his face to ward off the blows from the stones, from the knife that sticks him, slashing his fingers and his palms. He sees red against the faded stripes of his shirt, it's his favorite, old and soft, Brooks Brothers, lightly starched at the collar, and it's ruined.

"Stop," he gasps, "you're hurting me, why are you hurting me? Stop it, please, enough—"

The boy is in a frenzy now. Dancing around the man like a crazed rooster, breathing hard, screaming in Spanish, jabbing the knife in wherever he can, cutting, stabbing, and the other boy has grabbed the man's hands, squeezes the man's big hands in his own, sticky with blood, there is blood everywhere, until the man drops his head, drops *his arms, drops to all fours, where he sways, coughs, and topples to one side.*

"Enough," the man chokes as he hits the ground, and one of the boys (which one?) reaches out and tears the three-inch blade in a ragged line across his throat.

And then the man is swimming. Swimming underwater, swimming fully clothed, swimming against the tide, coming up from the deep, he can see the sky, red at the water's edge, if he can just reach the surface he'll be able to breathe.

Silence. No chitters. No chirping. A groan only, the faintest gurgle. Then, finally, the call of the mourning dove, but nobody hears her. The boys are already halfway up the ravine, gasping for breath, pulling themselves back up the hill to the traffic, to the world, with twenty thousand dollars and the man's car keys in their pockets.

28 | Uncles

All the things I'll never know, not just about his death, about his life! His childhood, his growing up, his marriages, his work, his friends; I tell myself he wouldn't have answered me anyway.

"What do you want to know that for?" he might have said, or, "I don't remember," or "Ask my mother," or maybe he would have shrugged and played with the remote control. I'm jealous now, of the life that didn't include me, and I comfort myself with the bits that are exclusively mine.

Nearly three years after I'd last seen Paul, three years since we'd had any contact at all, I muster the courage to call him at his office in New Jersey. His voice is flat on the phone, not just business-like but bored, as though I'm an unworthy job applicant, or somebody trying to sell something.

I'm nervous, short of breath, but I make my appeal, stumbling over my tongue, explaining that I've come to realize how little I really know about my father. I remember Paul wrote a memoir not long after the murder. Would he mail me a copy? Could I read it, please? I'll return it to him, of course.

"I don't remember writing anything," he says.

"You don't—but you said—I mean Gayle told me you finished a book. Submitted it to publishers. Don't you have a copy somewhere?"

"Gee, Dinah, I don't know."

It had been a terrible time. He'd gotten rid of everything having to do with the murder. Such an awful ordeal. Who'd want to remember? Who'd want to think about it?

"You got rid of your book?" I'm sitting on the floor, rocking back and forth on my knees. Unbelievable. *Unbelievable.*

He says he must have. He says he'll look around, if he finds anything he'll send it off to me. No pretense at further conversation, no politic effort, no *How's the family? How are the kids? Regards to your husband.* It can't be that he actually hates me, can it? Or more shocking still, is he completely indifferent?

A week or so later a small manila envelope arrives in the mail with Paul's return address. He's enclosed two copies of an obituary and an ancient bumper sticker, faded and yellow at the edges, from my father's bid for the U.S. Senate almost thirty years ago.

In November, 2001, I call Michael, who still speaks to me as far as I know, to ask if he will meet me in New York over the holidays. Michael's wife Meryl takes the call and says she knows he'll be happy to see me. Can I tell her what this is about? I want to know more about my father, I say, who he was as a boy, as a brother, as a son; who he was in his other life, the one that didn't include me. We set up a tentative date to meet and several days later I get a note from Michael in the mail; *Enclosed please find three photos of your father,* he writes. He adds that he's looking forward to our visit.

Two of the pictures I've seen before. I sent them to my grandparents myself. In the first my father and I are cheek to cheek, dancing at my wedding. Fifteen years ago I might have told you I had to have looked better that day than I do in this four-by-six-inch glossy. Whose idea was that haircut? Why did I think that dress was so special? But what rivets me now is the resemblance; we share the eyes, the wide-mouthed grin, the big cheeks, the high forehead, the well-delineated jaw. We smile, both of us, with our whole faces—not just eyes or lips, no—everything cracks wide open, crinkles and bends in our oversized skulls.

In the second picture my father holds Eliza and beams for the camera. I remember when I see it how he loved to pose with my children, how he'd whisper something to make them laugh and then lurch into focus looking straight into the lens.

The third photo is of my father in the White House, in the Oval Office, seated across from Richard Nixon and John Erlichman, both of whom lean forward in their chairs to better hear—as Michael remarks in his letter—what Nelson Gross, black-haired and not quite forty, has to say. Who is that man, so young, so handsome, so confident? *Who is he?*

The night before the day we've planned to meet, Michael leaves a message on the machine in my sister's apartment, where Fred and I are staying for two nights over the winter holidays.

"This is a message from Michael Gross for Dinah," he says. "I am hoping you will convey my intention to meet with her tomorrow in Manhattan . . ."

Good God, he's inherited the mantle, he's become my grandfather, a public speaker with a penchant for twenty-five-cent words.

Michael goes on to say that Paul wants very much to join us at nine o'clock the next morning at the venue of my choice. I call him back, incredulous, excited: Paul's coming? To see *me?*

"Oh please," he answers with warmth and, I realize now, astounding diplomacy (duplicity? Wait and be the judge), "please, Dinah, don't be silly. Paul and I will see you in the morning."

I'm determined to do this on my terms so I negotiate for an extra half hour to have time to buy myself a notebook and some blank cassettes at Woolworth's. Not only am I setting the time, I'm going to record the interview.

It's bitter outside this last day of December, but in my sister's one-bedroom, overheated and facing a brick wall, weather and light are superfluous unless you have to go out. In that case you need to turn on the radio, or, easier still, run down two flights to the foyer in your bathrobe—which is what I do— to determine the appropriate dress for the day. The sunshine jars from the bottom of the stairs, coming in through the frosted glass window in the heavy, steel door—painted brown and chipping—that leads to the stoop outside. When I open it a crack, the cold bites between my brows and brings tears to my eyes. I dress in black jeans and a gray sweater, clogs, a black felt fedora, and a borrowed down jacket. Fred looks up from the Sunday *Times* to wonder out loud if that's what I'm wearing. On the defensive, I answer with bravado I don't feel.

"Why not? I mean, it's Sunday morning, what *should* I wear?"

It's the weekend in New York City, is my reasoning, it's early, I'm meeting family for breakfast in a diner, am I supposed to dress up? Fred sniffs and goes back to the paper.

"Freddy. Do you think I should wear something else?"

He looks up, almost startled. "You look fine," he reassures me. "Geez, Dine, relax, you look fine."

My nose is red with cold (I catch my reflection when I bump into a mirrored pillar) as Fred and I enter Googles on the corner of Seventy-eighth and Second, an upscale Italian diner that serves a disappointing mound of long skinny fries with breakfast eggs instead of hash browns. I've brought my Starbucks with me—so as not to order so much as a cup of coffee—all churned up about who's going to pay for what, and besides, how could a person possibly eat at a time like this?

Michael, in pleated slacks and a suede jacket, greets us at the door of the restaurant and walks us back to a booth where Paul, seated already, nods his head and extends a hand to Fred. I lean across the booth to kiss his cheek and Fred says hello, good-bye. He has only come along to be polite, to provide moral support; he's on his way to the river and the Upper East Side neighborhood he remembers from before we left the city for Los Angeles, seventeen years ago.

I slide into the booth next to Paul and for more than a few moments, I am unable to speak. I'm breathing too fast, sweating under the arms and my hands are clammy. Arranging my coat and hat on the seat beside me, and rummaging for a notebook in my bag before I place it on the floor between my feet, I'm playing for time. It's been nearly four years since I sat in a room with these two; each time I've seen them since my father's death, I've been shocked by their stature, their physical presence, separate and together, two large men, tall, broad-shouldered, deep-voiced, big-faced, so like my father, but not my father at all, either one of them. This time, removing my hat, reaching for napkins, I cannot control my voice, and I ask them, wiping my eyes with the back of my hand, to forgive me, please, it will take a minute, just a minute.

"I can't get over what you look like," I try to explain, just as the waiter delivers a plate to Paul.

It's Paul who really gets to me. Paul—who resembles my father most—not so big, not handsome in the same way exactly, but reminiscent of the real thing. Where my father was severe and intimidating, Paul is pudding. Under other circumstances, before my father died, a person could have teased Paul and been rewarded with an embarrassed giggle, a self-deprecating glance. Chances are he was the child most poked and prodded; it would have been Paul who suffered the pinched cheek, the pat on the bottom, my grandmother's relentless fussing and prying, with the least amount of resistance; and we all assume, of course, that as the middle child, Paul somehow escaped her more negative obsessions, not to mention my grandfather's expectations and judgment. Paul, so like my father, but doughy at the edges. He's wearing a cashmere sweater, navy blue, over an oxford shirt. His eyes are long and narrow under unruly brows, but he parts his hair carefully to one side, and it frizzes a little at the ends, whereas my father, who had less of it, combed it straight back.

"Well now," says Michael, who is more fair, the towhead in the family albums, leaning back against the booth on the other side of the table with his legs crossed in front of him. "Why don't you tell us what it is we can do for you?"

The waiter reaches over me to put a plate down in front of Paul, a toasted bagel with Nova Scotia and a small tub of cream cheese on the side, capers, red onion, lettuce, and tomato, and Paul, visibly relieved to have something to do with his hands, begins to smear cream cheese across one half, licks his thumb when he puts down the knife, squeezes a lemon and says, "Sorry, Dinah, but I have to eat."

"Eat," I say. "Of course, you have to eat. It's breakfast, it's . . . of course you do."

Paul hunches over his plate, elbows spread wide across the table, bites into his sandwich, which he grips between the fingers of one hand, the other wrapped around the body of his coffee cup and not its handle which is turned away from his palm, as if it was too small for his big, hairy fingers. My whole life I saw my father's trembling hands as some glaring symptom of ill health or neurosis and now it turns out that Paul's hands shake, too. What a relief! This ailment is physiological and benign to boot. It wasn't due to rage or repression, or if it was, then Paul, too, must be repressed or in a fury, which now that I think of it, is absolutely possible. But no. More likely this is some genetic tic, a short in the nervous system, and I'm relieved. Glad, even. No matter that he's dead and gone, I'm happy to have this particular mystery if not solved, then revealed for the mystery it is. Because would two grown men express their emotional shortcomings in the exact same physiological way? Isn't that doubtful? Isn't it wonderful that all of a sudden, from this moment on, I don't have to worry anymore about my father's shaking hands as symptomatic of deep-seated anxiety?

Later it's Michael who brings up my father's trembling fingers. And Paul admits, with a shrug, that his hands shake, too. And when I ask if he knows why, he just shrugs again. Michael's hands do not shake, nor has he ever struck anyone as being repressed. Irrepressible is more like it, according to family lore.

They don't want to be taped. And for all my original conviction, my sense of purpose, I don't bother to argue. For one thing the restaurant is loud with conversation shouted at tables, between tables, from kitchen to counter to waiters across the floor, clinking china, cups against saucers, spoons against cups, clanking silverware, and Muzak in the background, it's hardly worth it to push the subject, and anyway, I haven't the will. These men, these uncles of mine, they are testy, they are wary, they are too strong for me. I open my notebook and pull the top off my pen. I explain that I want them to talk about my father as a boy, as a young man. What do they remember? What was he like at home? What was it like to grow up with him?

Michael, his father's son, a lover of stories, of jokes and speeches, launches in.

"Your father was a 'wunderkind,'" he says, placing his hands behind his head, looking up at the ceiling. "He was intimidating under any and all circumstances, even to his own father, *our* father," he says with a nod to Paul, "who simply could not force him to do anything."

Then he leans forward. "But perhaps I'm commandeering the subject. After all, Paul may remember more than I, and differently, he and Nelson being closer in age—"

"Dinah, let me ask *you* something," says Paul, laying down his knife.

"Paul and your father were closer than your father and I," Michael interjects, ever the translator, ever the mediator.

"I want to ask *you* a question," Paul repeats.

"Please," I urge.

"Why did you stop talking to me?"

"I didn't. I—"

"Just a minute here," says Michael.

"No, wait," I say, "I didn't stop talking to you, you stopped talking to me!"

"I never did," says Paul with his mouth full of bagel.

"You were angry with me," I tell him. "You advised me to get a lawyer, and then you got mad when I did."

"Your father botched that will," Paul mutters almost to himself. "God, what a mess he made of that thing, he broke every goddamn tax law in the state of New Jersey, and I was left with the whole mess, Dinah, the whole mess I had to clean up."

"You told me to hire a lawyer," I moan.

"You didn't trust me," Paul reproaches.

"Well, of course, I did, but you can't be all things to all people," I protest.

"Now, now," says Michael.

"I lost my mother and my brother and my father and a couple of dear friends in the space of a year or so," Paul says into his plate. "It was too much, Dinah."

I say that I'm sorry for him. And I remind him *his* brother was *my* father.

"I had no one to do it with, Paul. My mother couldn't help

me. My stepmother? Who? And I thought—stupid of me—but I thought, maybe you guys," I am looking from one to the other of them now, "maybe you guys would step in somehow, maybe you would love my children. And then," I'm crying now, "then you stop talking to me, and I have to do this thing alone, and listen, Paul, I *missed* you."

How did we get to the next part? I think Paul nodded. I thought at the time it was like some kind of thaw was setting in. Paul and I are not so different, really, both of us gentler versions of Nelson, himself, and we neither one us like being angry. I stowed my shredded napkin in my bag and asked the waiter for another. Paul finished his bagel. And Michael got us back on track.

"My brother Nelson," he said, "was a giant. Physically, I mean, he was gigantic."

"He wasn't a giant," disparaged Paul.

"He was enormous," Michael disagreed. "For God's sake Paul, he was at least six four."

"He was never six four," sneered Paul.

"He was."

"Never, he was never."

"All-American in high school, Dinah," Michael insists. "My big brother was a star. He was bigger than life."

"I think," I interject, almost apologizing, "I think I remember he was, like, six two."

"Six three at least, 225 pounds. At least," says Michael. "He played tackle, remember."

The truth is my father resented "extra-large." Once, for his birthday, I proudly gave him a polo shirt with the Izod label. I spent what I thought was a whole lot of money on what I thought he would deem quality merchandise. *I get it*, my present was meant to say; a demonstration of my understanding of the culture, the label thing, the preppy thing, the country club, Ivy League, dressing-the-part thing that I believed was important to him.

"I don't wear extra-large," he said. "Would you mind if I returned it for the right size?"

But his shoes were a 12E. Who ever heard of such a thing? And why did I inherit those big feet (just the length, not the width, by the way) and not his perfect vision? Or, come to think of it, his outsized self-confidence and drive? Where's the justice in that?

"You couldn't force him to do anything," says Michael. "His own father, *my father*, understand, couldn't make him. One time, Nelson was five or six, I think, just a little boy. According to my father he dropped something on the floor during a meal. My father told him to pick it up. He refused. And later, much later, when my father was trying to explain my older brother to me, he told me that story and he said, 'Michael, you should have seen the look on his face. Nobody, I mean *nobody* could ever make Nelson do anything he didn't want to do.'"

Isn't it peculiar, I register somewhere even as I listen to Michael, that he calls Grandpa, "*my* father?" Not "Dad" as you would expect him to under the circumstances. As in "Dad did this" and "Dad said that." But "my father." As though he was the favorite son. The heir apparent. Is this a testimony to the intimacy that my grandfather achieved with his youngest? Or is it just that these brothers were so isolated the one from the other, so exquisitely entitled in every way, they didn't even share the experience of their parents? Because, come to think of it, don't they all do that, doesn't Paul speak in that oddly possessive way about my grandmother? "My mommy" he would say, teasingly, in front of the others and "I visited my mother," I once heard him say to my father after having gone to put flowers on her grave on a Sunday afternoon. And didn't Nelson, himself, call Grandpa "my father" even in the presence of his own brothers? And isn't this what toddlers do before they are truly comfortable in the world? Before they have learned to share?

"My daddy says I can have a soda," Eliza told me when she was not yet three, as if I had no connection to "her daddy" at all. As if I hadn't been well-acquainted with him long before she, come to think of it, but thanks very much for clearly identifying the progenitor in question.

But then I reject this line of psycho-babble or at least dismiss it in its endless ramifications—for hasn't Michael also called Nelson, "my brother" even with Paul sitting across from him in the booth, stirring a pack of Equal into his second cup of decaf? "My" is more than just proprietary, it's powerful, it's connective, it's a rightful claim on history and humanity and grief. It is a word that underlines our loyalties and loves and the inevitability of pain and loss.

"Nelson would walk into my office. We worked together, understand."

I want to know when, and Michael explains they were partners for three years, when he was twenty-five and fresh out of law school, and my father was thirty-two years old.

"He'd walk into my office with a brief in his hand. He'd start speaking on his way in the room, like nobody else was talking or thinking about anything else. No 'excuse me' or 'hello' or 'have you got a minute' none of that. Listen, even later, he never called, he never made an appointment. He just walked in. Wherever he went, he walked in like he owned the place."

I'm remembering now that well into adolescence I was reproved for talking on my way into a room. It was a sign of pathological self-involvement, my lack of awareness that anything of any interest or importance could be going on in a room before my entrance.

"He'd come in, give me instructions about something or other, like, 'take care of this idiot, get rid of this bastard,' that kind of thing. And then he'd leave and turn off the light on his way out the door. I'd be sitting at my desk. 'Nelson!' I'd shout after him. 'What? Oh. You don't need that light, do you?'"

Was he cheap? I wonder. Or completely narcissistic? Or just unconscious?

"I never understood my brother," Michael leans forward. "I agonized over it. We worked together. Couldn't he have been a little more cordial? My father tried to explain it to me. He said, 'Michael, listen to me, your brother wouldn't cross the street to say hello to his own mother.'"

Hearing this, I remember I'd often thought it would have been easier for him to be pleasant, to feign interest. I remember wondering if his wasn't a calculated indifference, if it didn't take a certain amount of effort. It wasn't laziness on his part, oh no, it was an exertion of power and ego. I'd wished more than once he'd say hello and good-bye to my grandmother when she came to take me off his hands for a couple of hours. And as I got older, I looked for ways to get a rise out of him, so bored was he, so jaded, so unwilling to engage. I teased him about it, flattered myself he found my candor entertaining and novel in a world full of people who had long since stopped surprising him.

"His temper was explosive," Michael says. "Once, he nearly throttled a judge over a traffic ticket. Nearly strangled the guy."

He was violent? My father was violent? My husband has told me to ask if he ever had a gun.

"Never," says Paul. "Nelson never owned a gun in his life."

I'm relieved.

I want to know if he was popular. In high school.

Paul nods that he was. "Because of sports," he says. "He was never Mr. Nice Guy, understand. But he was always a sports hero."

"Was he interested in all that? Being popular?"

"Absolutely," Paul nods. "Always. He was always doing that social-climbing stuff."

Can they tell me about my mother? About the courtship and marriage and divorce? About me?

"She was a beautiful girl," says Michael.

"Very pretty. Your mother was very pretty," Paul agrees.

"Were they in love?" I ask. "Did he love her?"

"I always felt," Paul says, not looking at me, "I always believed your father felt more strongly about you than he did about either of his wives."

That night I call my cousin Lauren, Paul's daughter, to whom I used to be close and with whom I haven't spoken since the brouhaha over the estate.

"Dinky," she says, "I heard you had a meeting today. The whole family's buzzing about it. How did it go?"

And she explains how Michael tricked Paul into coming to see me.

"Manhattan gives my father the hives," she explains, "so Michael calls him and says, 'You're my only brother, I want you to do something for me.' And my dad says, 'What, Michael? Whaddayawant?' And Michael says, 'I'm meeting with Dinah and I want you to come with me.' And Dad says okay, he'll come and Michael says meet me at the office at eight. And Dad shows up and says, 'So where is she?' And Michael says, 'We're meeting at a coffee shop, you drive,' and they drive to this place near the bridge and Michael runs in and gets them both a cup of coffee and comes back to the car and Dad says, 'So? Where is she?' And Michael, says, 'Here, here's your coffee, we have to drive into the city. Blah, blah, blah.' Because, I swear, if he'd told Dad you were meeting in Manhattan, he never would have gotten in the car in the first place."

We've been sitting in Googles for almost two hours. We've talked circles around what happened to my father on that September morning five years ago, and we are no closer to any kind of understanding.

"Why do you think it happened?" I search their faces. "How could it have happened like that?"

Paul sighs. "I can't think about it anymore," he says. "I gave up trying to figure it out."

He rises from the booth, and I slide out to give him room. "Come on now, Michael, that's enough; I want to get going."

I gather my belongings and button my coat and follow them out of Googles to the corner of Seventy-eighth and Second where we wait together for the light to change.

Michael puts an arm around me. "It's good to see you, Dinah," he says.

I thank them for coming.

"Paul," I blurt, impulsively grabbing his arm, "please don't be mad at me any more." My breath is fogging up my sunglasses. He shoves his hands in his pockets.

"Nobody's mad."

And then the light changes. Paul starts across the street. I yell out good-bye and he raises his hand without turning to look back. Michael waves and shouts over his shoulder that I should take care of myself. He follows Paul at a clip, not so much to catch up, I think, as to make it to the other side before the light changes again. My father's brothers cross away from me, and I turn on my heel and walk fast in the other direction, so as not to have to lose sight of them when the Sunday morning traffic starts to move downtown.

29 | Recovery

Cracker decides not to replace me, not to shoot my scene on Wednesday, September 25, the day my father's body is found. The producers send me a beautiful basket of flowers and a sympathy card.

"They waited for you," my manager tells me the day after I return to Los Angeles.

We do a night shoot the following week, wardrobe, makeup, producers and actors tiptoeing around me as though I'm horribly handicapped in some way, which of course, I am.

"I remember your father," says the star of the show. "I remember his place, that boat on the Hudson. He was a politician, wasn't he?"

Turns out this actor grew up in New Jersey. But I've forgotten how to make conversation. I only want to stand close to him, to put my head on his shoulder; there are no words to thank him for talking to me about my father, for knowing my father's name.

When a person dies, there are weeks and weeks of sympathy and concern. Then the rest of the world goes back to normal, and the bereaved remain under water, inexplicably breathing, uncomfortably suspended, looking up from the bottom of the deep, but unable to swim; not drowned exactly, but not of the real world either. Look at me, I'd shout if I could, I'm under water here, dive in, save me, or wait for me, at least, until I'm able to float to the surface.

I wore my father's tie pin for a year, so that people would ask, so that I could tell. I owed him that much.

I do something silly in the car, make some corny joke, and there's Jake in the rearview mirror, his half smile, his furrowed brow, an expression so specific, skeptical but engaged, dubious but game, it translates every time to, *What, are you kidding? Are you crazy or what?* It's a look I know so well. I saw it on my father's face, and I've felt it on my own; the muscles moving in a way that isn't learned so much as programmed, deeply familiar, historical even. I'll regard someone in amused disbelief, and I'll think, dear God, it's the *face*, I'm wearing it, Dad's singular grimace all over my countenance. I laugh out loud in thrilled recognition when I see it—the *face*—staring me down from the backseat of the mini-van. And then I stop abruptly: Is it all right to laugh? To be happy? Entertained? With my father dead only a couple of weeks?

At dinner parties I am the woman whose father was murdered. This renders me fascinating. I tell the story over and over. Eventually I can tell it dry-eyed, I can soothe my audience, assuage their horror, explain that I'm okay, mostly, that life goes on. It takes two years to attend a social gathering without talking about him. And just over two years after his death, we're sitting around a crowded dinner table, very lively, when my friend, the hostess, squeezes Fred's arm and says in a whisper, "She's back!"

A young woman comes to coach with me for an audition to play a detective whose brother had been killed years before in a tragic accident. In the scene something funny her partner says reminds her of the brother's sense of humor. The script calls for her to tease the partner and then to well up and confide that her brother is dead. But the emotion isn't working—it's forced—and it doesn't make sense.

"My sister died five years ago," says the actress. "I know what this feels like."

My instinct tells me she wouldn't cry on the job, and I say so. When you've lost someone you love in an untimely fashion, eventually it becomes your obligation to take care of your friends and acquaintances, to let them know you're okay. Well, of course, if someone is particularly moved, or horrified, or kind, maybe it all comes up again for a minute and a half. But mostly I don't cry anymore. I acknowledge the event; this was terrible, this wasted me, tore me up and down for a while, I explain, but everyone has a story, am I right?

For such a long time I thought my father's death the most interesting thing about me. But the truth is, nearly six years later, I don't think so any more. I'm very obviously focused on my children, my husband, my present, my future. My father's death belongs to him. He's the victim—he's the tragic figure—I am an ordinary, middle-aged woman trying very hard to be happy with my remarkably unremarkable lot. Not that what happened to my father doesn't inform who I am to some degree, not that I don't believe in the value of accumulated experience. (If I didn't think it all added up to something I'd be more inclined to lie about my age. But I always wonder, which years to lie about? Which part of my life am I prepared to say I didn't do?)

Still, considering how violent, how shocking it was—the murder, I mean—I am strangely unscathed. There was a time when I woke up with it every morning, went to bed with it every night. But even then my father's death wasn't allowed to overwhelm me because I do have children, because they were so young when it happened, because I couldn't fully submerge myself in the tragedy and take care of them too.

I wear my father's murder way under my skin. My circumstances forced me to push it down, and I'm glad. Glad for the complications of family life—actually glad for laundry and carpool and brown bag lunches—glad to live three thousand miles away from the mayhem, relieved that my children are healthy and secure by virtue of their ignorance, even though they're growing up in a scary city during scary times.

My friends defer to me as if I know something they don't. When their parents die they apologize—*after what you've been through*, they say, or *I don't want to bring up bad stuff for you*—as if their loss wasn't as terrible, more terrible, perhaps, than my own.

One woman loses her father to a heart attack, another to murder. The first woman grew up with her father, saw him every day until she left for college, say, moved back to her hometown as a married person, had dinner with him only two nights before he dropped dead. Woman number two grew up with her mother and her stepfather and a bunch of younger siblings and saw her father for a weekend here or there and for extended time at Christmas and over the summer. She moved clear across the country ten years before he died where he visited her a few times a year, and she never really resolved her ambivalent feelings about their relationship. How to quantify the loss? How to measure it? Not even having factored in their different personalities, it seems to me it can't be done.

My husband's mother died of cancer long before I met him. He was too young to lose her and too young to be married at the time (to somebody else) and sure enough, his first marriage unraveled in the face of her illness. He was his mother's caretaker; he watched her disappear into her disease. He fed her and bathed her and carried her to bed at night when she asked his permission to go to sleep. Surely he was more attached to his mother than I ever was to my father. Still it doesn't occur to us to lie to our children about the way Grandma Anne died. We don't go into details, but we don't lie. We haven't been straightforward with the kids about Pop because the truth is devastating, the truth is the stuff of nightmares, because a person never recovers from that kind of truth. Until she does.

Strange how when you don't say good-bye, you have a hard time believing a person is gone. Even now I cannot believe my father is dead, except that I haven't heard from him in such a very long time.

Over and over we do our days; we rise, scramble eggs, squeeze juice, go to school, to baseball practice, to piano lessons, bicker over homework and green vegetables, bathe in bubbles and fall into bed. Not so oddly I measure my father's absence by how much the kids have grown. Not by my own deepening crows' feet, or failing right knee, not by the crick in my neck or the twelve gray hairs that used to be three, not even by my growing acceptance of myself as a grown-up woman. No, I measure his loss and the length of days since I saw him last by how Eliza looks in a black skirt with her hair twisted up on top of her head, how she sings out the melody to "Take Five" on her alto sax, by how Jake pores over the sports pages in the morning, and handcuffs me with a spin serve to my backhand when I have the advantage. When I really see my children for who they are, for who they are becoming, that's when I miss my father most of all.

30 | Keeping in Touch

So, Dad, Jake made the All-Star team! It's not just that he's skilled, which he is, but he's only ten, and he sees the whole court. He knows where and when to pass. He's a team player, Dad.

Oh listen, listen to this, the other day? He was singing "Kumbaya." You know, the folk song: "Kumbaya, my Lord, Kumbaya . . ." I was telling him to do something—I don't know what, to brush his teeth or read his book or something—and he sings, "Someone's bothering me, Kumbaya." He's funny. He's just so funny.

He's tall, Dad. Tall and lean and his hair is like wall-to-wall carpeting. And he's got your eyes.

And Eliza is beautiful. Not like me at all, you were wrong about that. She's skinny—all legs—she's built like Fred, lucky girl. She's a star in school, Dad. Wants to be a lawyer, she says. Or a director. Or a writer. She's got a mean forehand. Punishing, honestly. And you should hear her on the sax, Dad. When she started, I swear, it was as big as she was, but now she just wails on it, plays on the deck outside her bedroom, and the dogs in the valley howl back at her.

And she gave up the horses, which is just as well, I mean, who could afford that, anyway? Although I tell myself you'd have helped—with the riding, or with schools—but who am I to say, I mean, maybe you'd have laughed at me, right?

I talk to my father sometimes. In the park. There's a stretch of dirt path, no more than a hundred yards or so, leafy and green even in the middle of summer in Southern California, muddy with enormous puddles after the winter rains. The trees, big and gnarled, reach to each other from either side. To the left, the hill slopes up, thick with shrubs and tall grass and butterflies, tiny birds and skittering lizards, rustling invisible creatures. To the right, it plunges down, the incline so steep, I can't help think of my father, my father in his dress shoes. . . . The path curves there, aesthetically, as though it was painted, so lush, so remote, you forget you're just above Glendale, just north of downtown Los Angeles, minutes from the Police Academy and Dodger Stadium.

I talk to my father in that place. Not just because it reminds me—the severity of the drop—and not because that's where I saw him last on that morning in May, 1997, when we jogged together before he showered and left to catch his flight back to New Jersey. It's quiet there. It's protected and private. For a few moments, maybe, I talk to him out loud like he's perched in some tree, an enormous head, looming in the sky with the moon in the morning, waiting for me to catch up just beyond the curve. At first the words ring out odd and flat—so I lower my pitch—then I realize, I don't have to project. So I speak normally until my voice peters out, until I'm talking in half-phrases, whispering, finally just barely moving my lips, just thinking a conversation. No, not a conversation. He doesn't answer me. Or, at least, I don't hear him. I'm not especially gifted that way; spiritually-challenged more like, and my father is dead. Still, the first time I did it? The first time I spoke to him? It was so real, I brought tears to my own sentimental eyes.

I believe and I don't. If he lives on, isn't he omniscient, doesn't he know everything already and what business have I putting my spin on things? Or is he completely disinterested in our progress here on earth, in the flesh? Has he transcended worldly love and concerns? Does he watch over us or is he bigger than that, smaller than that, no part of that, whatsoever? I can't think too long or too hard about it. I tend to follow absurd lines of reasoning when I try, like A, he's just dead, forget the afterlife, okay? Or B, he exists on a plane you can't fathom and he's no longer connected to you and yours. He just isn't listening.

"Mom," asks Jake when he is nearly nine, "what do you think happens to you when you die?"

"I don't know," I answer and explain there are many different theories, religious and otherwise, but that really nobody knows for certain whether or not there is an afterlife.

"Here's what I think," he interrupts. "When you die, you get born again, a new baby in a new family, and you just can't *remember* who you were before. So what I want you to do, if anything happens to me, Mom? I want you to put a note on me, so I'll know who I really am."

Roxy, our chocolate lab, was riddled with tumors by the time she turned twelve. Her back legs didn't work very well anymore. She had cataracts and she smelled sick and sour and then, finally, she stopped eating. Fred took her for a walk in the park on the last morning. He threw a tennis ball for her, and she limped over and picked it up and brought it back to him and put her head in his lap. Then he and I took her to the vet, where we watched a doctor give her an injection; her eyes never left Fred's face, she shuddered, and then she disappeared. One minute she was in the room and the next she was gone. I looked for a light, some shimmering evidence of her existence in the here and now, but I didn't find it, of course. Beside us was a carcass, an old, brown shell of a dog, but Roxy had left the premises and gone where? Where do we go when we die? How to label a person, make a secret marking on a soul so as to keep track of where it's gone and how it's doing? So it will know where to come back and visit in case it forgets.

It is not the interpretation of dreams that's brilliant, I think, so much as the dreams themselves.

I tell my husband I dreamed about my father the night before. He was waiting for me at the country club. Waiting on a vast verandah overlooking rows and rows of tennis courts laid out like a giant game board, perfect squares of red clay bordered with green, and I was late because I couldn't decide what to wear. I knew my father was exasperated. I knew he was checking the time, biting his thumb, twirling the grip of his racket in his right hand, thinking about making a phone call. If he got on the phone, I'd lose him for sure, but nothing fit, I was just too fat. I was late, so late, and I looked like a cow in a striped and pleated tennis skirt. Then, suddenly, I was in the Body Shop, looking for a cure for an ingrown toenail. In the dream, ingrown toenails were fatal, of course. The Body Shop offered me some sort of syrup in a small green glass bottle. Swab the toe with a drop or two of this, said the salesgirl, maggots will breed between the flesh and the nail and eat the nail away.

Sometimes it's just a pleasure to wake up in the morning. I'm not so fat, and I don't even own a striped tennis skirt. My toenails, if slightly ingrown, are under control, although having recently trimmed my son's a little on the short side, my anxiety isn't hard to trace.

I don't remember the dream until later in the day. Fred and I are driving to dinner somewhere when I mention it.

"I dreamed about my father last night."

"What'd you dream?"

"I was keeping him waiting. We were supposed to play tennis. I couldn't find anything to wear."

"Too fat," Fred says knowingly.

"Yup."

"What do you think it was about?" he asks.

"I should probably get back to work," I say, craning my head to see if there are any decent chairs on the walk outside my favorite Sunset Boulevard junk shop. We're in the market for kitchen chairs.

"What do you mean?" Fred asks.

"I should get my ass in the chair," I say. "I should be writing about my father."

I brace myself, expecting my husband to raise one brow, the hypocrisy of me, not to mention the hubris, for haven't I admitted that I don't believe in this sort of thing? In ghosts or in messages from the great beyond? And even if I did, even if I've changed my mind, the nerve to presume my dead father would appoint *me*. Anoint me. Actually rely on me to get any of it right. As if he wouldn't know better, wouldn't know the account would have to be more about me than him in the end. But Fred doesn't wince or flinch or even pause before he answers.

"He's waiting for you," he nods.

That night, lying in bed in the dark, before I reconnect with the dream current, the big swell of my own subconscious (my dreams, episodic in nature, seem to follow one another night after night like waves coming into shore), I remember the maggots, the toenails, the Body Shop cure. It must have to do with my father's remains and the way they were delivered. Ashes, death, maggots, death, and the solution, the secret of life, there all the time, waiting to be resurrected from the bottom of a brown paper bag.

Meanwhile, Fred is taking a playwriting class at UCLA extension. He's a skeptic, my husband the screenwriter, hates nothing more than group spirituality, prescribed moments of silence and collective revelation. He hails from no-nonsense East

Coast Yankees and the Protestant work ethic, even though he's a creative type. Simon, the enlightened teacher of Intermediate Playwriting 101, has conceived the course from a New Age perspective, so the first third of the three-hour class usually makes Fred a little uncomfortable. He doesn't much like exercises designed to open his soul and tap into his unconscious or subconscious or even conscious-but-purposely-veiled agenda.

But he does come home with one interesting practice.

"This one could be helpful to you," he suggests, since I profess to be struggling with why I am writing. Articulating a reason, a motive, a larger point or theme has got me stumped.

"Simon says," Fred explains (can you believe it? *Simon says*), "to put your protagonist on a stage all by himself and ask him what he wants. You ask, you answer in character, out loud, or on paper. Go ahead, make him tell you. Make him tell you what he wants!"

A woman enters. An actress, that is. Mid forties but she looks good in a black dress, above the knee, but tasteful, and she's wearing black hose with Lycra, the kind that are supposed to pull you in, shape you up, so nobody can see the wrinkle in the skin just above the knee which is the reason women over forty should abandon shorter lengths, unless they're wearing black hose. Anyway, black dress, black hose, black heels, she stands in front of the curtain, red velvet, of course, and starts to sing.

No. This isn't cabaret. This isn't musical theatre. Ask her what she wants.

VOICE FROM THE HOUSE: Hey, lady. What do you want?

ACTRESS: Huh?

VOICE: What do you want?

ACTRESS: What do I want? Whaddayamean what do I want, is this a trick question? Shit. What do I want. I want somebody to come to my house and wash my windows. Water my plants. Polish, polish, polish. And dust. I want a new car and a new coffee table. I want enough money to send my kids to private school. I want enough money! I want . . . I want to lose five pounds. I want everyone to be nice to me. I want everyone to love me! I want to be smarter and better and younger. I want some control, some control over something, anything, you know? What do I want. I want one more conversation with my father. I want—

VOICE: Wait a minute.

ACTRESS: What?

VOICE: That last thing you said. About your father.

ACTRESS: Oh yeah. Well, my dead father, I mean. The one that's dead.

VOICE: So what do you want to talk about? With your father, that is.

ACTRESS: I want to ask him how he is. If he is. I want to tell him about my kids. I want to tell him about me. I want to say that I miss him, that I'm not going to forget, that I'm trying to remember, to help the kids remember, that I wish he'd come back to us, send us a sign, that I'd like to make him proud, I want—I want . . .

VOICE: Go on.

ACTRESS: I want him to know how grown-up they are. We are. I want him to see us all grown-up. I do.

She exits.

A ghost enters. A big, strong ghost in khakis and a polo shirt, thinning hair, good physique, large head. If he's wearing a straw Sombrero with a hole in the brim he takes it off, hangs it by its leather string off the back of his chair and sits, legs spread wide, stretches his arms behind his head, breathes deep, closes his eyes against the sun.

VOICE FROM THE HOUSE: Hey. Hey, Mister. Talking to you from the last row, sir. Can you tell me, is there anything you want?

GHOST: *(Peering, squinting into the house)* What? Who is that? Who the hell is out there?

VOICE: I am, sir. I was asking if you have any idea what you want.

GHOST: None of your business, moron.

VOICE: Don't be like that. Do us a favor, will you?

GHOST: What?

VOICE: Tell us what you want.

GHOST: I don't want a damn thing. I have everything I want.

VOICE: C'mon now.

GHOST: Get lost, buddy.

VOICE: Mister, please. If you could cooperate this one time . . .

GHOST: *(sighs, shakes his head)* What do I want. I want good weather. A good day on the course. A free ride and a decent meal. A nice bottle of red wine. Oatmeal for breakfast. Crackers. I want some crackers. Or peanuts. You got any peanuts? I'm hungry, for chrissakes, I'm always hungry. No, no, forget it, don't give me the peanuts, I don't need them. Look, you want to know what I want? I want to lose five pounds, Jesus, I have to take off five pounds, you know? *(He massages his elbow.)* I want somebody to fix my golf arm. It's my elbow, right here, see, never bothered me before and now it won't let up. Hey, I'll tell you what I don't want. I don't want to get old, that's for sure.

VOICE: Stick to the question, will you, Mister?

GHOST: *(softer, with a chuckle)* What do I want, huh? Well, I'll tell you. I want to see my grandchildren. When you get to my stage in life, what else is there, anyway? I want to see those kids grow up, that's what I want. That's something to stick around for, you know?

31 | Family Gifts

When I was still in college, for one of my birthdays, Nelson
and Noel gave me a Cartier watch. I was totally bowled over. I
knew so little of labels and their price tags, I didn't realize how
preposterous the real thing would have been. I just thought,
finally, a gift worth having, not some hand-me-down bottle
of perfume, not some recycled sweater, and I wore it all the
time and people were suitably impressed, and then one day I
got pushed into a swimming pool with the watch on my wrist
and it stopped, of course, so off I went to repairs at Cartier.
Where I was told that the watch was a copy, a fake, the sort
of thing you can buy on the corner of Madison and Forty-sev-
enth from a guy who also sells ties or socks or sunglasses. And,
sense of entitlement unshaken, I confronted my father and his
wife, who snickered at me for thinking they would ever have
given me the real thing.

"But you never said it was a copy," I protested.

The tacit message was: why would we ever buy you a real
Cartier?

Which incensed me. Why would they? Because they could!
Because I deserved it! Because who the hell would want to
wear a fake one?

I always thought I'd lose my stepfather first. He was older than my father by more than five years, and I just assumed. I assumed that my younger siblings would be fatherless, and that I would have this *other* father, and that no one would understand the extent of my own grief over Ron, a "step" after all, and that I would not be thought as sympathetic as they, as bereaved as they, since I'd still have two living, breathing parents. I imagined that I would feel guilty and disconnected and apologetic for having a father when they didn't, regardless of the roles the two men had or hadn't played in my upbringing.

May, 2002. Per my request, my stepfather FedExes an envelope full of pictures in anticipation of his seventy-fifth birthday. The ones dated from 1927 through the '60s are sepia-toned, or black and white and faded. I've also asked for his favorite pictures of his grandchildren, all four of them. He has no idea what I want with any of the photos, nor do I, but he enters into the spirit of the thing, agrees to be feted in whatever way I see fit. I am the mother of two of those grandchildren. I am his eldest child, and I will be the mistress of ceremonies. I only know how important all this is to him when I get to the bottom of the envelope. He's enclosed a copy of his birth announcement, a spoof on a new building inspection, since his own father, who died of heart failure when Ron was eighteen, had been an engineer.

Entrance (reads the inspection): *Thirty-two teeth missing to be filled in at the appropriate time.*

I'm tickled to discover that Ron's parents were so whimsical, so witty, so obviously young and full of beans in May of 1927. Like nothing else, this announcement brings them to life for me, puts a face on the grandfather I never knew, and italicizes the girlish spirit, makes sexy and smart the woman I remembered best as "Gramma," the Queen of Scrabble and Go

Fish, Our-Lady-of-the-Sofa-Bed, wrinkled and tart as a beach plum with white hair, false teeth, veined, muscular calves.

I hire a stretch limousine for the occasion. And a photographer who arranges the photos into still lifes on her kitchen table, climbs on top of the adjacent counter and takes pictures of the assembled collages, to be copied and presented as souvenirs of the event. I choose between restaurants and menus and wines and kiddie meals and purchase odd tokens for the party bags: dental floss for everyone over thirty and jellybeans for the children, all four of them. I order seventy-five gem-toned balloons and flowers for the tables at Café Pinot, which sits adjacent to the public library downtown, and a cake from Sweet Lady Jane on Melrose, which I cancel later, too bad about that, since the odd-looking whale of a confection that Café Pinot constructs will taste like wax, but by then we will all be completely satiated and nobody will care in the least.

"What are we doing for Dad's birthday?" I'd asked my sister on the telephone, way back in April.

We had finished an early supper and the last of the day's light was waning. Only the weekend before it would have been dark by now, but just last Sunday we'd turned back the clocks, and now there was a stripe of light from the corner window along the back of the living room sofa, lingering on a bowl of oranges in the middle of the coffee table, throwing a shadow across the food section of the *Los Angeles Times*. In New York City it was nearly ten o'clock at night. My sister was wearing pajamas, I imagined, sitting on an angle in her wicker sofa, flanked by a standing lamp with a carved white base and her desk on one side, and a dresser full of clothes on her left, the television on mute, every light turned on. For her, it was nearly bedtime.

"I mean seventy-five, for God's sake, what are we going to do?"

"I don't know," Jill answered. "I honestly haven't given it any thought."

"No more power tools," I said.

She agreed.

"Will there be a party?" I tossed the food section to the floor and crossed my legs over the arm of the chair.

"I doubt it," she answered, "That's not his kind of thing, really."

I tried to imagine my stepfather in the middle of a room full of people, a little puzzled, frustrated, actually, not to be able to get on with his day, his garden, his evening, his book.

"We should get him a tree," yawned my sister, and I imagined her pulling a striped afghan over her knees, propping her feet up on the trunk that does double duty as a coffee table.

"Like they do for dead people in Israel?"

"Come on. I mean a fruit tree or something, for the farm. He likes that sort of thing."

"Okay," I said, on a sigh, and not too long afterward I hung up and went back to Eliza and her book report and Jake and the C-sharp minor scale and the mountain of laundry on the dining room table.

Several days later my mother called midmorning from the apartment in Larchmont to say good-bye. They were off to Italy for a two-week tour of Palladian houses, churches, and bridges.

"Have you thought about Dad's birthday?" I asked her, huffing and puffing. I was pedaling hard at my life cycle, reading an editorial about anti-American sentiment in Europe.

"Not really," she laughed.

"It's a big one, Mom."

"It is." I imagined her balancing the phone between her left ear and her shoulder, chopping parsley for a stuffed breast of veal with a great big chef's knife, since for her it was well after lunch and time to think about dinner.

"Jill thinks we should buy him a tree," I panted, "like they do for dead people in Israel."

"What Daddy would really like is to have his family around him," said my mother.

"And that's impossible," I said, wiping my face with my shirt sleeve.

She agreed.

I told her to let me know if she came up with a spectacular idea. I told her to be safe.

"We will," she said and hung up.

While they were touring Italy, I was on simmer about the man's birthday. How many times does a person turn seventy-five, I asked myself? A tree didn't cut it. I was irritated that we couldn't have a party with a zillion guests. That we couldn't give him a week for two in the British Isles. That we couldn't buy him a sports car. That we couldn't do something extravagant, excessive, and momentous. Never mind that all of the above would only have embarrassed him. That it wasn't his style to make a big fuss. I wanted to do better than a tree. Never mind if the grand gesture didn't appropriately reflect his or any of our values, particularly. I wanted to make it.

My parents returned early from their Italian adventure. The weather went bad, and my mother caught a cold she couldn't shake. In New York State the temperatures sailed up into the nineties and Ron, looking out over a canal in Venice, obsessed about his garden in the Berkshires. About what was popping and what wouldn't ever pop if he couldn't get to it with a spade and a hose and a pair of clippers. They drove up to the country the morning after they arrived back in the States, which is where I reached them early the following day.

"Listen, Mom, I'm having trouble getting behind this tree thing," I said. "I know you just got off a plane, and my timing isn't great, but hear me out, okay?"

Admittedly it made no sense for Joe and I to travel east with our respective families for a birthday celebration smack in the middle of the school calendar. Instead, I cajoled her to fly herself and my other two siblings to Los Angeles, where it just so happened Ron would already be on business.

"Let me turn off the bath," she said, and I imagined her, in a blue and white checked caftan, walking the old wide boards, painted green, from the bedroom to the bathroom, where she would have thrown some bath oil, Secret of Venus or White Linen, into an oversized tub, now full and steaming and ready.

She got back on the line to say that this was a splendid idea. She would help me recruit the ranks.

Jill, who teaches preschool in lower Manhattan, jumped on board the party train like a shot. As long as someone else was paying the airfare, she'd find a way to be there.

My brother Joe, from his cell phone in San Francisco, was more reluctant. Did his reticence have something to do with our actually living in the same time zone? No suspension of the imagination, no catching him at a good time of day, his time is my time, and I imagined him sitting at a table outside Peet's Coffee with his cell in one hand and a cigarette in the other. He had just planned a long-awaited canoe trip with friends on the weekend in question.

"Tell your friends to change the date. Tell them your father will be in LA for his seventy-fifth birthday. Tell them you have to be there. Your crazy sister says so. Just tell them."

"I'll see what I can do," he equivocated.

But my brother Andy was the real monkey wrench. He works for the City Council of New York and May is when they determine the yearly budget. He had to make himself available every day, all day, even weekends, or he'd lose his job. He couldn't make travel plans in advance and even if he could come, his ticket would wind up costing upwards of a thousand bucks.

"This is nuts," he told me, after a rash of e-mails. "I just can't make this happen."

I've never seen his Brooklyn studio so I couldn't imagine him on the phone, in a room, in a chair, standing at a counter; instead he existed for me like some big head with his bearded chin close to an equally disembodied receiver.

"It was a good idea," my sister said when she heard the disappointment in my voice.

"I'm so pleased that you thought of it, dear," my mother said. "It's just such a big country."

"We'll do something else some other time," Andy called back to say. "You're attaching too much importance to the actual date," he added.

I didn't hear from Joe, but I imagined he was relieved.

That night after supper, as I was pouring leftover puttanesca into Tupperware and Fred was loading the dishwasher, I told him, "It just can't be done. We're getting him a tree."

"Well, you tried," said Fred. "You made a good effort."

"It just seems so wrong," I complained.

"What would you have done for your father's seventy-fifth birthday?" Fred asked.

"I'd have gotten there," I said. Knowing in a flash that at best I'd have been an invited guest, at worst, deliberately excluded; and then I scold myself since the thought is unfair and almost definitely untrue. In fact I'm sure my presence would have been demanded as his due. Not just my presence, but that of my children, who legitimized me somehow in his eyes, and I'm happy for a moment to imagine my father, who died before his sixty-fifth, summoning me, in gruff tones, to his seventy-fifth birthday party.

"I expect you," he would have said. Of that I was suddenly certain. Abruptly and absolutely convinced.

We'd have attended the affair, and he'd have been proud to show us off. But I would not have orchestrated the event, which would have been grand, I imagine, altogether out of my league. I knew not to insinuate myself in my stepmother's life if I could help it. I knew not to intrude on my father's real family, on the people with whom he sat down to dinner most nights, my stepmother and their son.

Fred's implication was that I was overcompensating. Doing for one what I wasn't able to do for the other because he was dead. But that wasn't it, it was something else entirely. Yes, I was determined to do something for Ron, but no, it wouldn't have been my place to do it for Nelson had he lived. In truth I'd been trying to win a permanent place in my stepfather's heart for as long as I could remember, long before my real father died. The place was mine, it had always been there, I had nothing to prove, but I kept trying anyway.

Isn't it fascinating? His real children, his legitimate three, would have liked to make this party work if they could. But even if they couldn't, they were still his children, he was still their father, just as he was before this anniversary. *I'm the eldest*, I told myself, *it falls on me to coordinate the party*. And *I'm his stepdaughter*, I told myself, too, parenthetically, as if that was merely incidental, when in fact I was bound and determined once and for all to establish our relationship as just as thick as blood.

I'd all but given up on the party when Andy called again to say he'd arranged to come in on a red-eye Friday night and return to New York on Sunday morning.

"So it's happening?"

"It's happening."

"For real?"

"Make your plans."

Joe called that same afternoon to say that he and his kids would drive down the coast the day of the party. Did I have room to put them up that Saturday night? You bet I did.

I whooped. I danced on the coffee table, which had belonged to my father-in-law and was commissioned from a carpenter in Maine to withstand, no, even better, to *inspire* a woman to dance.

When my sister arrives, the day before everybody else, we wrap party favors, buy champagne, taste cheeses, and come home with exotic olives and caper berries from the local gourmet shop. At five o'clock or so Saturday afternoon, everybody gathers in my living room, all dressed up. My mother opens a box full of velvet party hats from Venice, and we cavort to the strains of Brubeck and Etta James and Chet Baker and Ray Charles while the photographer snaps away, roll after roll of film: Sam, Joe's four-year-old, just a face, a cockeyed smile in the middle of a conspiracy of balloons; Charly, his sister, somber, big-eyed, wearing a hat nearly as tall as she; My own Eliza, smiling close-mouthed so as not to reveal a mouth full of metal; and Jake, perfectly at ease in a blue blazer and tie, as though his favorite garb wasn't oversized basketball shorts and a T-shirt full of holes. Each of them and each of us with Grandpa somewhere somehow, not posed, not contrived, but when the film comes back a couple of weeks later, there we are, this big, slightly extended family and its patriarch.

So there's a glitch or two. We leave the aforementioned slab of cake to the waitress at the restaurant with no compunctions at all. The food isn't fabulous, and I'd ordered altogether too much wine. Silliest of all, the limo service calls a half an hour before takeoff to say they've lost their stretch to another gig, they're sending us a Hummer.

"Call them back and tell them forget it," says my mother. "I wouldn't be caught dead in a Hummer, no way, no how."

"But Ma—" I protested.

"Dinah, really. A military vehicle? My God. How inelegant."

We save ourselves three hundred bucks and take two cars. I do drive a mini-van, not elegant exactly, but it's handy with a crowd. The point is, glitches are okay. A person counts on a glitch here and there for the sake of the story.

When my father died, my siblings, these three from my mother's second marriage, were paralyzed. Miserable for me, anxious for me, but unable to mourn with me and consequently tongue-tied.

But this I will never forget. Not long after the memorial service—before the shock wore away, before grief dug in its heels and did its strange, unsettling work, before the silences, the awkwardness, the estrangement in varying degrees, and the slow work of returning to myself—my brother Joe called one afternoon to check in.

"I want you to know something," he told me on that day early on. "Since I was a little kid, people would say, 'Ooohhh, so Dinah's not your *real* sister, she's your *half* sister, right?' And I'd say, 'Yeah, I guess so, whatever.' But I never knew what they were talking about. I mean as far as I was concerned, you'd always been there. You were my sister, my big sister. *Half* sister? It just didn't mean anything to me. I didn't think about it like that. Until these last few weeks. And now here you are going through this thing, and we don't know what to do for you—"

His voice broke and I felt the heat rise up in my face. I started to say something about how I understood, but he interrupted me.

"What I want you to know is when you get through this thing, Dine, you have a whole family waiting for you. A *whole* family. That's what I wanted to tell you."

I want to be taken for granted; at least I think I do. So I'm embarrassed to receive a gift certificate in the mail from my brothers and sister a week or so after the party.

"Stop your whining," says Fred. "You'd have done the same for one of them."

Joe, Andy, and Jill have pitched in to treat me to the Beverly Hot Springs, a day spa only a couple of miles from home. The entrance fee includes use of the waters, steam, and sauna, and the "Body Care" coupon involves enthusiastic pummeling and scrubbing and a milk and honey bath. They'd heard from Fred that I liked the "treatment" at the Korean spa—no nonsense and completely anonymous—and they wanted to let me know they'd enjoyed the weekend.

"You really pulled it off," my mother tells me on the telephone.

And Ron writes a letter that he ends with, "Thanks for the memory. Love, Dad."

I'm pushing my sister to move to California. I think she spends too much time with my parents. I think she's settled way too early for one so young. She's only thirty-three years old but she's just about given up on men. She lives with a dog named Barney and she eats Szechuan takeout off pretty blue and green plates from Crate and Barrel maybe three nights a week. On weekends she drives up to the country, hitches up her jeans, rolls up her sleeves, puts on her gardening gloves, and digs in Ron's vegetable garden, makes vats of homemade red sauce with Leah, and visits local swap meets and junk shops to peruse for treasures in the late afternoons.

"My life isn't so bad," she assures me.

"Well, it isn't so good either," I say. And she doesn't argue.

"I can't leave them," she insists.

"You can," I tell her. "You can, you should, you must."

To her father, our father, I say, "You have to push her. You have to give her permission to leave New York. She thinks you don't want her to go."

And then I lower the boom:

"You remember," I say, "you did me a tremendous service almost twenty years ago. You told me I had to get out of my rut, shake things up, make a change, get away from Mom—"

"That was different," says Ron. "That was a different situation."

"Dad, for whatever reasons, for so many reasons, you were able to be objective about me in a way that you aren't about her. She's in a rut. She's spending every weekend with a bunch of old people in upstate New York."

"As an alternative," he says, "as an alternative to being alone and all cooped up in an apartment in the city."

"Exactly," I say. "And what kind of alternative is that?"

"I hear you," he answers.

Eliza knows I want my sister to leave New York. She knows I think Ron is unable to be objective about his youngest child. She wants me to explain the difference between objective and subjective parenting. Am I objective, she wants to know, about her? Not always, I admit. I tell her I have to watch myself. I have to be careful not to invest disproportionately in her triumphs and her failures. I have to let her be her own person. It's rare to have an objective parent, I explain. We parents have to work at that sort of thing.

Eliza considers. She decides, finally, that I have had the optimal upbringing. And I wonder if she isn't right.

32 | After Life

According to my mother, this writing is my inheritance, my father's posthumous gift to me.

"This is your exorcism," she says.

We were so sure when our children arrived they looked like one of us or the other. But then the resemblance shifted, wandered, amorphous, over their little faces. We chalk this up to the factor of the undecided gene. How else to explain how it is that my daughter, who, until she turned three, was a fairer version of me, now indisputably mirrors the photos of her paternal grandmother? And my son, whose baby pictures were interchangeable with mine (we pulled out snaps from 1959 and dubbed them "Jake in a dress"), now begins to resemble his father, ruddy and lean with a suspicious amount of cartilage between the tip of his nose and the top corner of his eyebrows. He favors my mother, too, Jake does, exotic bones in a heart-shaped face—but then, my mother always said she and Nelson were taken for siblings. No argument, though, Jake has the eyes, those unmistakably Asiatic windows, narrowing to slits above his cheeks, all mischief, all glee, stunningly familiar even and especially when he was missing two front teeth and laughing open-mouthed.

Why do we want to have children? It's unthinkable that they should have to take care of us in our old age, especially when we've no intention of getting old. But don't they insure our legacy here on earth? Even so, we're compelled to accept each child as different and separate from us. Which doesn't mean we won't continue to find comfort in genetic evidence of immortality.

My hands are large. I can comfortably stretch just over an octave on the piano. Studying my own sturdy fingers—big knuckles, short nails—I tell myself my hands look capable at least, they can cook and garden and make music and rub a sore neck, untie knots, sew buttons, soothe, stroke, dig, and polish. Like the rest of me they are strong and serviceable.

My daughter has graceful hands. Her fingers bend, dance, curve at the joint, and I realize one day with a shock they are shaped like my sister's, their hands are identical, Jill's and my Eliza's, and this means they have to have come from my mother's family, since she is the parent we biologically share, although—get this—my mother's hands are much more like mine.

There! A connection! And a riddle, too! Where did they come from, those beautiful hands? Who's having a shot at the only life after death I can begin to understand? We've no idea, any of us, they're exclusive to the girls, my sister and my daughter, and they bring me closer to them both by bringing them closer to each other. They suggest responsibility, a link to the past, a promise in the future, a chance that my sister will find something of me in her own child. As for my daughter? Well, we have never seen these hands before, and now we will never stop looking.

Search for ripples, reverberations, resonance and you'll find it most of the time. So Saturday morning four years ago, Jake, at five, is playing soccer with his teammates at the Elysian Fields Recreation Center, burned out grass, weeds, dead dandelions, no shade, sky like an overexposed photograph. My little boy runs down that bleached field dressed in red nylon shorts and shirt, tall socks, shin guards, and cleats, a miniature pro, like something three-dimensional against that flat, still backdrop. He grins at us, squinting into the sun, sticks his index finger in the air to let us know they need just one more goal for victory. Fred and I wave back, cheer, whoop, find each other and freeze, overwhelmed, both of us, by the resemblance, and Fred only says one word. *Nelson*. The tears actually do spring to my eyes. It is not just that my son looks like my father—it's that I am not the only one who sees this; my husband is my witness. There he goes, galloping in the other direction, shooting the goal with all the joy and exuberance of the moment, that's the one, that's him, my father's little ticket to immortality.

But this is too much to ask of Jake. A big, unrealistic load to carry. And, anyway, what about the other ancestors? All those other shades, if they exist, ought to rise up about now with a reprimand as in, *Hey, Hey, just a minute, we've got purchase here, too. You think you know, you think you see, but you don't get the half of it, the confluence of cells, of genes, of history perpetuated in your children, you've no idea, none at all.* For what are the hands, my daughter's hands, my sister's hands, if not proof of some laughing spirit, some mystery soul wafting overhead on a whispered, *They belong to me, they're mine!*

33 | A Pretty Good Day

It's been five years since I saw Stuart Rabner, who prosecuted my father's case for the state of New Jersey. Although I expect no less of him, I'm gratified when he remembers my name and takes my call. Once I've got him on the phone, I admit I've been writing about my father. I'm warm, sincere, even cheerful with Stuart; it's important to me that he understand this isn't a morbid preoccupation. I'm serious about getting it right, that's all. I've called to ask for copies of the original confessions. I hasten to add that my book is a memoir. It's about our relationship. I don't want to spend time inside the minds of the murderers, nothing like that. But I'm trying to be thorough, and I'm looking for anything at all that might deepen my understanding of what happened. Stuart promises he'll investigate and let me know.

Several days later, he calls me back. The videotaped confessions were never transcribed as far as he can tell and are not a matter of public record. I can request them under the Freedom of Information Act, and he'll make them available, but he cautions me to consider carefully before I do.

"Listen," he says, "I do this for a living. After a while, you deal with this stuff all the time, you forget the individuals, you know what I mean?"

But my father's case he remembers well, and he doesn't think I want to "open that can of worms."

The confessions were detailed, he tells me, and the way they were delivered, "without affect," in his words, cost him "more than a few nights' sleep."

"Think about it," Stuart says. "Let me know what you decide."

"You don't strike me as squeamish," says a friend who thinks I ought to view the tapes.

"I'll watch them first if you want," says Fred who means to be generous, but his offer grates.

I'm not afraid of the tapes, and nobody's viewing them before I do. When I write the government for permission, it never occurs to me my appeal will be denied. The boys were minors when they confessed; the Freedom of Information Act protects their interests in this case, rather than my father's or mine. I wheedle and plead, but Stuart is unwilling to let me see them in the privacy of his office in Trenton. "I'm sorry, Dinah. I just can't do that. I can't."

I owe Stuart Rabner one more call. He was unfailingly generous and kind, and I should say so. Thanks to him in part, I've read everything that was written about my father's death, and I've had the opportunity to speak with the men who apprehended his killers. I was present at the sentencing and I have a transcript of the proceedings.

No tape will bring my father back to me. No tape will tell me what I want to know. It's my father I long to see and hear, not the boys who took his life.

I should let Stuart know I don't need to see my father's murderers again, on videotape or anywhere else.

When we finally tell the kids, it's not at all as I'd imagined. I leave the big brown file deep in my closet, tucked behind a pair of old gardening clogs and a shoebox stuffed with receipts from last year's tax returns. It's a Friday evening in June, not yet dark, but it's not like we've got the whole day ahead of us either.

How could I have thought the clippings, yellowed and brittle and no less shocking with the passage of time, would be useful to Eliza or Jake in this particular instance? How could I have believed that bright sunlight would diminish the enormity of my news?

When I decide to do something, I simply cannot wait. This goes for large appliance purchases, elaborate cooking projects, home repairs, and letters to the editor. Fred, luckily, isn't nearly so impetuous. Particularly with regard to big-ticket items, his good sense prevails. He tempers my enthusiasms and pulls gently on the choke chain. For several months now Fred has quietly wondered every so often if the kids shouldn't be told the real circumstances of my father's death. Even so, my pronouncement at dusk on this day in early summer seems abrupt to him.

"You want to tell them *now*?"

"Yes."

"You don't want to think about it?"

"No. Now."

"What about tomorrow morning?"

"No. We've got the whole night together. The whole weekend. I'm ready now."

At long last I've acknowledged it's getting weird, this big untruth, this black hole in their short life histories. Fred loosens the collar and gives me my way.

We convene around the coffee table.

"We want to talk to you about Pop," I say.

"What about him?" Eliza asks, concerned.

"About the way he died," I answer.

"I remember," Jake announces. "He died in a car accident. Right?"

"No," I say. "You're old enough now to understand what really happened. Pop was murdered. He was kidnapped in his own car and killed for money."

Eliza sits up straight in her chair.

"But you said . . ." She folds her arms on her chest. "Who else knows about this?" she demands. It's all she can do not to stamp her foot. She wants to know why she wasn't clued in sooner, and she struggles, fiercely staring me down, to remember exactly what she was told almost six years ago.

"So you lied to us?" she accuses.

We defend ourselves. We didn't lie: we omitted information, but we didn't lie, we'd never lie about something so important, we promise. We remind her she was seven years old when it happened, and Jake was four.

"I knew it," she says. "I knew there was something I didn't understand." She is talking to herself, working it through out loud. "Jake was too young," she says, staring at her hands in her lap. "You couldn't tell me because you couldn't tell Jake."

And then, in frustration, she asks, "Why did you have to tell us tonight? Why did you tell us at all? Oh Mom, why did this happen, why did this have to happen to Pop?"

Now the kids want to know about the killers, where they are, when they will be released from prison, and I realize, they're frightened.

"What do you think about them?" Eliza asks. "Do you wish they were dead?"

"No. I don't know," I answer, trying to be honest. "I *don't* think about them. They can't hurt us," I add, in an effort to soothe and reassure.

I used to fantasize, improbably, that I would sit across from one murderer or the other on a crosstown bus in Manhattan twenty years from now. I would be about my father's age at his death, and the killer would be not much older than I am now. Maybe we'd brush elbows when one or the other of us descended at Eighty-sixth and Broadway. Maybe we'd even mumble a word or two—*Sorry, excuse me*—but neither of us would realize the link, feel the snap of the line stretched between us, severed with the yank of a lever, the whoosh of closing metal doors, the groan of the bus as it pulled away from the curb. This, however, is not a fantasy I choose to share with my children.

I was hoping to avoid the details, but Jake, perched on the arm of Fred's chair, eyes huge, unblinking, asks, "How? How did they kill him?"

"Oh honey," I say, "they did it with a knife."

He dissolves in that moment, his cheeks go red, and he starts to cry, silently at first, and then he sobs, "Why? Why couldn't they have used a gun? Why did they have to do it like that?"

Jake and Eliza, the believer and the skeptic, each child is bound to break my heart on a daily basis. Jake, brimming with trust and empathy, because he expects the best of the world; Eliza, confounded by reality straight from the womb, because she smartly suspects that nothing in life can possibly meet her high expectations. His righteous indignation in the face of injustice, her righteous anticipation of the same; how will I ever equip them for survival?

I remember my own preoccupation, as an adolescent, with death and destruction. I was a sucker for tragedy, obsessed with Anne Frank and certain that every growing pain was evidence of cancer, a harbinger of my own premature demise. I read John Gunther's *Death Be Not Proud* over and over and waited for my very own brain tumor to rise up out of my scalp. Not so Eliza, who refuses to read anything about the Holocaust and frowns on the most propitious of ambiguous endings. Her days are fraught as it is, she might argue in her own defense, a parade of hormonal episodes from which she emerges unscathed and humiliation-free only a percentage of the time.

"I wish you hadn't told us," she blurts, folding her arms across her chest. "I was having a pretty good day."

"I'm glad you told us," Jake says a few hours later, tapping his toothbrush on the sink and heading across the hall to his bedroom. Exhausted, he pulls the covers up high and inclines his face to the wall, cool against his cheek. "I might have to wake you guys in the night," he warns, "if I have a bad dream or something."

"Mom?" Eliza calls from her room after I've told her good night. "Mom, can you come in for a minute, please?"

I head back into the dark and sit on the edge of her bed.

"I just wanted to tell you," Eliza says, "it's good that you told us, Mom. You did the right thing."

34 | Coda

I've called and left a message for my mother about silk flow-ers. On impulse I bought an entire bouquet. Long-stemmed. Really beautiful, I think. But my husband is appalled when I clue him in to the fact that the arrangement he's admired over by the fireplace is permanent.

"Fake flowers?" he snorts. "You bought fake flowers? Ugh. They're—they're for old people. Blech. Fake flowers. Disgusting."

"But you thought they were real."

"But they're not."

In matters of taste and design I always defer to my mother. She who would not be caught dead or alive in a Hummer.

Eventually she calls me back.

"Silk flowers," she says with authority, "can be lovely. The trick is to do it right, dear. Don't let them get dusty. Put them in a vase with a bit of water in the bottom. Make sure you have an adequate amount of foliage. Live foliage is a good way to go. Tell Fred," she adds, "that silk flowers can be a strong element in the best interior design."

I'm about to say good-bye when she asks, "Dinah, dear, do you want to be adopted?"

"What?"

What did she say? Oh God, don't tell me, she knows someone who knows someone in LA, she's got a job idea, a mentor idea, some cock-amamie career proposition, what can this be?

"Do you want to be adopted?"

"Adopted?" I ask stupidly.

"Now that this is all over, I mean. Now that Nelson is dead. And you've gotten through this thing. Daddy always wanted to adopt you, you know. He would have—"

"Mom, I'm a grown woman. I have two kids of my own."

"So?"

"So, no. No, thanks. That's so kind of you. But no, I don't want to be adopted."

"You don't want me to ask Daddy about it?"

"No. No, Mom, I know who I am. I know who Dad is. I'm okay. Okay?"

"All right, sweetie," says Leah.

And we both hang up.

The guy who directed *Peter Pan* that long ago summer in Whitefield, New Hampshire, what was his name? It was a nonequity stock production. We were a bunch of kids living in a farmhouse, with no budget, no frills, and only a week's rehearsal before we put the show into repertory with *South Pacific* and *Deathtrap* and *Cabaret*. How would our off-off Broadway director stage the flying sequences, we wondered, and I, for one, was grateful to be double-cast as Mrs. Darling and Smee and not to have to run about the stage with my arms stretched out like a kid playing Superman in her parents' backyard. But this guy whose name I can't remember came up with a brilliant idea. Each of the flying actors, Wendy and her brothers and Peter, too, had a shadow, a stagehand dressed in black, choreographed with the others to lift their respective actors and dance them through space. The convention worked even better than wire. It was less literal and organic to the piece, the premise being that Peter returns to the Darling's home to retrieve his prodigal shadow in the first place. The idea was thrilling in its simplicity and so wonderfully theatrical, too. Anybody can hang a wire from the ceiling. But special effects pale alongside human invention. And use human invention—the imagination, that is—to light up a fundamental truth and you might just hit the universal nerve; who of us in the world has not, at one time or another, been mesmerized by some aspect of her shadow? Night after night, performance after performance, we actors held our breath in the wings and waited for the moment when those shades came to life, for the audible gasp of collective recognition and awe.

Nothing like motherhood to tweak one's sense of oneself as a daughter. And nothing like a parent's death to put a person in touch with her own mortality. But it's one thing to come to terms with the facts of life; the fear that grew in me after my father was killed was something else entirely. So crushed was I, so shaken and afraid, I believed I would die, too. Not in due course but soon and under violent circumstances.

I'd take a little too long to hike the old familiar loop with our dog, Sully, for instance. The sun would drop like a big orange melon behind the hills to the west, the sky would glow red and turn purple, and suddenly it would be too dark to be walking alone in an urban park just above downtown Los Angeles. A man would jog toward me, or a man would appear suddenly from behind a grove of trees, or a man would intercept me on the path with his own pack of dogs, and I couldn't help thinking, *Here it comes, one of these guys is going to cut my throat and leave me here to die.* I'd fantasize Sully in a frenzy, sniffing and licking and barking and finding his way home in the dark. Fred, getting in the car to come look for me. Calling the police. Finally, sometime after daybreak, I imagined, they'd recover my broken body, a visible lump in a tangle of mustard brambles, no blossoms now, just a skeletal scrim under the hot summer sun. People would shake their heads at the tragedy. Knifed in the park not long after her own father was murdered. Left alone to die, just as he was.

Even in the mornings, under a cloudless sky, I was fearful. Afraid to make eye contact with anyone on the trail, I lowered my gaze, became well-acquainted with my smudge of a shadow, squashed, deformed, always slightly ahead of me on the long, dirt path. I acknowledged our connection—she was I, I was she—dwarfed and cowering before some unnamable, unknowable assailant.

And then, not all that long ago, I noticed as I strode up the hill that my shadow was long, boldly outlined and purposeful. A confident shadow. You'll shake your head, maybe. You'll say my shadow is a function of the physics of weather and light and hasn't anything to do with my state of mind. You'll tell me this here is a different season, a different time of day. You will remind me that I'm seeing with different eyes now, and you'll be absolutely right. The shift in time and season and the way we look at our personal landscape is part and parcel of recovery. And we are recovered, my shadow and I, or, if not recovered, then having taken things in stride for the moment, we are tall.

IN THE AMERICAN LIVES SERIES

University of Nebraska Press

Also of Interest in the American Lives series:

Fault Line

BY LAURIE ALBERTS

In 1969 Kim Janik was a young man shining with promise who was in love with Laurie Alberts. Twenty-five years later, when Kim's naked and decomposing body was discovered on the Wyoming prairie, one photograph—that of the Harvard junior and the seventeen-year-old—was found in his abandoned car. This is Alberts's attempt to piece together what happened in between.

ISBN: 0-8032-1065-5;
978-0-8032-1065-3 (cloth)

Hannah and the Mountain

Notes toward a Wilderness Fatherhood

BY JONATHAN JOHNSON

Longing for a home in big, wild country that would keep them passionate and young, Jonathan Johnson and his wife, Amy, set out to build a log cabin on his family's land in a remote corner of Idaho. But what begins as a doable dream suddenly looks quite different when, on their first morning in the cabin—without electricity, a telephone, or running water—the couple learns that Amy is pregnant.

ISBN: 0-8032-2601-2;
978-0-8032-2601-2 (cloth)

In the Shadow of Memory

BY FLOYD SKLOOT

In December 1988 Floyd Skloot was stricken by a virus that targeted his brain, leaving him totally disabled and utterly changed. *In the Shadow of Memory* is an intimate picture of what it is like to find oneself possessed of a ravaged memory and unstable balance and confronted by wholesale changes in both cognitive and emotional powers.

ISBN: 0-8032-9322-4;
978-0-8032-9322-9 (paper)

Order online at www.nebraskapress.unl.edu or call 1-800-755-1105.

Mention the code "BOFOX" to receive a 20% discount.